A
Practical
Guide
To
Fly
Tying

Written by Bob Gerding

Photographs by Kurt Kubie

Cover Photo by Dick Kent

Published by: Fly Fishing Fantasies Ltd.
12212 Sierra Grande NE
Albuquerque, New Mexico
87112

DEDICATION

To my wife Harriet. My partner and greatest supporter in whatever I may decide to do next. My love of fly tying and fishing is overshadowed only by the love of our life together.

ACKNOWLEDGEMENTS

My first "thank you" must be to you who have purchased this book and are taking time to read this page. I have skipped over far too many acknowledgements in books I have read. Believe me, these people are important.

First to my students from whom I have learned most. I salute you for challenging me.

Next to my employers who have had incredible understanding concerning this project. Charlie and Barbara Domenici have been supportive and understanding of my effort and time requirements. It's nice to have your employers become real friends.

Next to those people who actively supported this project.

Kurt Kubie, the master photographer and devil's advocate. Kurt devoted many hours to my project. I was privileged to watch a master at work in the sun, studio and darkroom.

Dick Kent who very graciously shared his studio and incredible knowledge.

Don Murphy and Tim Rademacher, who listened as friends and gave sound advice.

John Ferguson, who took me by the hand and led me through the perils of printing.

My family, who put up with long hours and short tempers.

Finally, my parents, who while no longer here, provided the spark to fire my interest in fishing.

TABLE OF CONTENTS

TABLE OF CONTENTS

Who Me?   An Introduction to Tying Your Own Flies

Congratulations! I'm happy to be the first to welcome you to the fascinating world of fly tying. Yes, you! You can tie your own flies.

For those of you fortunate enough to have some experience, a special welcome. I hope the existing pleasures of tying your own flies multiply. While this book begins at an elementary level—I start with step 1 and progress—I'm sure you will learn more than the true beginner.

Let me set you at ease. First, fly tying is not difficult. An illusion of difficulty surrounds this "art" and is encouranged by many fly tyers. When you find how easy it really is, you will kick yourself for not starting years ago. You may feel that your big, clumsy fingers could not possibly work with something quite that small, or perhaps your eyes are not what they used to be, and you are concerned with visual acuity. Believe me, if my fingers can tie, anyone's can, and fine vision is not necessary.

I hear many reasons why someone starts tying his own flies; economy is certainly among the leading reasons. Other reasons are the need to tie some pattern at streamside to tempt that afternoon's fussy trout or the desire to adopt a pleasure-giving hobby. Whatever reason you have for starting, I am sure the reason you will continue to tie your own flies is the pleasure gained by tying patterns that, not only satisfy the artist in you, but the fisherman as well. Pride and pleasure—a highly sought-after combination—often proving elusive in other hobbies.

Fly tying is a hobby that combines the pleasure and relaxation of tying with the immensely satisfying result of catching trout on your own hand-tied flies. Fly tying will make anyone a better fly fisherman because he or she will have a better understanding of flies, their origin, and how they should be fished. It has been satisfying and rewarding for me not only to tie flies, but teach people the techniques used in making their favorite flies. I am pleased to share with you these techniques which I hope will add another dimension to your fishing pleasure.

I have tried to present the tying techniques in the same manner and order as if you were in one of my classes. The descriptions are detailed. Pictures and illustrations are included to show techniques graphically. This detailing of basic and advanced tying techniques has evolved over years of teaching and research.

This work is not intended to be a pattern book. There are many currently available to you, and I feel it senseless to duplicate them. I have included fourteen patterns to illustrate different techniques, and I have chosen these as a solid representative collection you can comfortably fish in almost any trout water. I do not mean to imply that these are the only patterns that will work, for there are literally thousands of choices. At the end of each pattern chapter, there are dressings listed for four additional flies using the same techniques covered in that chapter.

If you will begin with the Wooly Worm and progress to the Humpy, you will develop and perfect the techniques necessary to tie almost any of your favorite patterns. Concentrate on the techniques involved in each pattern, and learn to recognize them. I have summarized the techniques for you in the materials chart.

While these techniques have evolved over the years, the sources are varied. I have tried to give credit to obvious sources; however, it becomes impossible for me to remember where I learned many of these techniques. If I slight anyone, I apologize and plead only my poor memory. As a matter of fact, I can take very little credit for any of these techniques.

Bob Ferding

MATERIALS

Selecting the Best Materials

Once basic techniques are learned and practiced, the difference in flies boils down to materials. The selection and handling of materials separates the good fly from the mediocre fly.

Care should be taken, therefore, to select the best materials. How can you do this without years of experience? You are going to have to rely on another's expertise until you have gained your own. The ideal source would be a local sporting goods shop close to your home that carries a full line of fly tying materials and equipment.

If you have no local sources, there are several good mail order houses. Do not hesitate to explain fully to them, when ordering, just what you want, even to discussing patterns and sizes. The sources I recommend for good, reliable fly tying equipment and materials are:

Charlie's Sporting Goods
7401 Menaul NE
Albuquerque, New Mexico 87110
(505) 884-4545

Buz's
805 West Tulare Avenue
Visalie, California 93277

The Orvis Company
Manchester, Vermont 05254
(802) 362-1300

Randal Kaufman
Streamborn Flies
13055 SW Pacific Highway
Tigard, Oregon 97223

Bud Lilly Trout Shop
West Yellowstone, Montana 59758

The materials necessary are listed on the materials chart and can easily be obtained from any good source. If any problems arise, call me at Charlie's Sporting Goods, and I will attempt to help you any way I can.

MATERIALS

Brown Neck, Grizzly Neck, Cream Neck

Brown Saddle Hackle, Golden Pheasant, Black Saddle Hackle

Mylar Tinsel (wide & narrow), Lead Wire, Red Floss

Turkey Quill, White Duck Quill, Peacock Herl

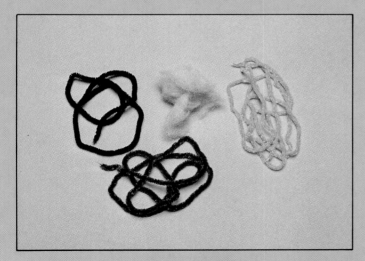

Yellow "Poly" Material, Brown Chenille, Black Chenille, Yellow Chenille

White Calf Tail, Muskrat Fur, Hare's Ear & Mask, Light Elk Hair, Deer Hair

TOOLS

Crest

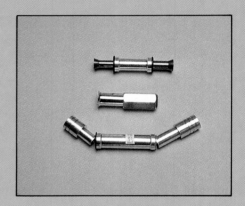

Price Jr.

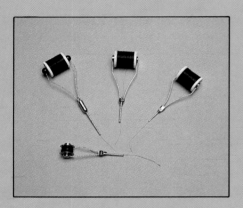

Thompson, Crest, Matterelli,
Matterelli Midge Bobbins

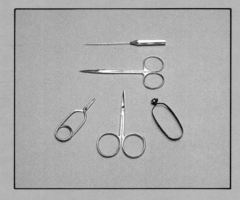

Dubbing Needle, Surgical
"Iris" Scissors, Orvis Long
Nose Hackle Pliers, Orvis
Scissors, Thompson Duplex
Hackle Pliers

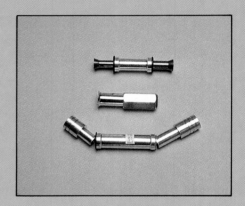

Hair Stacker

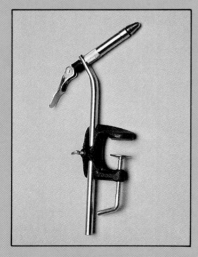

Thompson "A"

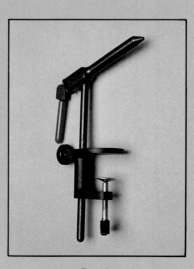

Orvis

MATERIALS

Materials Chart

No.	Fly	Technique
1.	Wooly Worm	Basic Body and Palmer Hackle
2.	Montana Nymph	Basic Nymph Form
3.	Peacock Nymph	Fore and Aft Hackle
4.	Grey Hackle Peacock	Standard Wet Fly
5.	Rio Grande King	Wet Fly Quill Wings
6.	Muskrat Nymph	Standard Dubbing and Lead Wire
7.	Gold-Ribbed Hare's Ear	Loop Dubbing and Wing Covert
8.	Brown Bivisible	Dry Fly Hackle
9.	Grizzly Mosquito	Standard Dry Fly Proportion
10.	Adams	Hackle Tip Wings and Mixed Hackle
11.	Elk Hair Caddis	Hair Wing Tied Down
12.	Royal Wulff	Upright Hair Wings - Wulff Style
13.	Muddler Minnow	Spinning Deer Hair - Basic Streamer
14.	Humpy	Combining Hair Techniques

Category	Material	1	2	3	4	5	6	7	8	9	10	11	12	13	14
Hooks	Mustad 79580	✓	✓	✓										✓	
	Mustad 3906 B				✓	✓									
	Mustad 9671						✓	✓							
	Mustad 94840								✓	✓	✓	✓	✓		✓
Body Materials	Brown Chenille	✓													
	Black Chenille		✓			✓									
	Yellow Chenille		✓												
	Peacock Herl			✓	✓								✓		
	Yellow Poly Material											✓			
Feathers	Brown Saddle Hackle	✓													
	Black Saddle Hackle		✓												
	Brown Neck Hackle			✓		✓			✓		✓	✓	✓		✓
	White or Cream Neck Hackle								✓						
	Grizzly Neck Hackle				✓		✓			✓	✓				
	Mottled Turkey Wing							✓						✓	
	White Duck Wing Quill					✓									
	Golden Pheasant Tippet				✓	✓									
Furs & Hair	Muskrat Fur						✓				✓				
	Hare's Ear and Mask							✓							
	White Calf's Tail												✓	✓	
	Light Elk Body Hair											✓			✓
	Deer Body Hair												✓	✓	
Miscl.	Narrow Mylar Tinsel							✓							
	Wide Mylar Tinsel													✓	
	Red Floss												✓		✓
	Lead Wire						✓								

MATERIALS

Body Materials

Chenille — the same material used to make bedspreads, rugs and other fluffy fabrics. The chenille used in fly tying must be of the *best* quality. Usually it can be obtained from a fly tying material supplier or shop. You will be disappointed in chenilles available in yarn or fabric shops.

Peacock Herl — the individual fibres (or barbules) on a peacock's tail quill. Again, the best and least expensive way to buy this is from a fly tying material source. The individual herls are usually stitched at the bottom making the bundle much more manageable.

Poly Material — may come in many forms, from a sheet to yarn, or even fluffy prepared dubbing material. If colors desired are not available, check your local yarn, fabric or embroidery shop for supplies. Poly is an abbreviation for polypropolene which is a very common substance for today's yarns.

Feathers

Saddle Hackle — comes from a rooster or gamecock and is from the part of the bird where you might imagine a saddle would be placed. These feathers are very long and relatively narrow. Usually of fairly reasonable quality in terms of minimum web and usable length of the feather. Saddle Hackle is used most often for palmered flies (i.e. Wooly Worm) or large wet flies. The best Saddle Hackle, while of good quality, is much too large to use on dry flies.

Neck Hackle — comes from the top of head, back, sides and front of the neck of a gamecock. The rooster most often is skinned with this patch laid flat and dried. When you buy a neck you are buying that piece of skin with the feathers still attached. Neck hackles are available in small packages of feathers only, however these are usually of poor quality and very expensive compared to a full neck. Neck hackle is used because the barbules are shorter than saddle hackle and much more adaptive to smaller (size 10 and smaller) flies. A good neck can be expensive; however, it will provide a large number of feathers to tie excellent dry flies. There is *no substitute* for quality hackle.

Necks are usually sold in three grades.*
A: Dry fly quality—barbules stiff and feathers going down to at least size 16 or 18.
B: Dry fly quality—not as good as an A and the feathers run usually larger.
C: Wet fly *only*—poorer quality (usually larger feathers. Excellent for wet flies).

*May be graded as #1, #2 and #3.

MATERIALS

Feathers cont.

Buy neck hackle *only* from a source you trust or has come highly recommended. You can be stung very quickly in the area of purchasing materials. There are also necks which are not graded and you have to buy these based upon your own, or someone elses, expertise.

Quills — usually wing feathers, or in some cases, may be tail quills. The two types of wing quills are primaries, which must be matched right and left; or secondaries which need not be matched, since the quill is in the center (more or less) of the feather.

Special Feathers — like the Golden Pheasant Tippets (which come from the neck of Golden Pheasant) are used for special color and effect. They are most easily purchased in small packages containing only a few of the feathers.

Furs and Hairs

All furs and hairs are self descriptive. You can easily purchase small patches of skin with the furs or hairs attached. I would not recommend buying full hides, since they will probably cause storage problems and may never be used.

One caution when buying furs. Some furs are recycled coats or scraps from furriers. If you want *only* the soft underfur that's fine, but for most uses you want the stiff, guard hairs which are removed when prepared by furriers.

Miscellaneous Materials

Miscellaneous Materials — Again these are self descriptive. My only recommendation would be to buy from a good reliable source. Quantities and qualities of tinsels and flosses may vary greatly and it's always nice to get your money's worth.

TOOLS & EQUIPMENT

Good quality tools produce good quality flies. If a tyer has to constantly fight his tools, the frustration will outweigh the pleasure of fly tying. While tools of tying are the most expensive part of any starting kit, good quality tools will last for years. The essential tools are:

1. the fly tying vise
2. bobbin
3. hackle pliers
4. dubbing needle or bodkin
5. hair stacker

I will describe the essential quality of each tool and recommend specific products.

The Fly Tying Vise

This tool is the most expensive and the most important. The vise *must* hold the hook securely without damaging the wire, point, or barb. It must be able to accommodate different sizes of hooks and be easy to use. The vises I recommend are shown on the color page of tools. The most expensive is the Price Vise, and the least expensive is the Crest.

The Bobbin

While there are several good bobbins, there is only one I would rate as excellent. The Mattarelli bobbin is the best. Look for the initials "FM" on the brass spool holders. Crest also makes a good bobbin, as does Thompson.

Hackle Pliers

The Thompson Duplex, with rubber and brass heads, is the most practical beginning hackle plier. It is easy to open and yet holds hackle tips securely. A good hackle plier should be large enough to hold comfortably in your fingers while wrapping hackles, but not so large as to be cumbersome.

A second choice for the best hackle pliers is the Orvis "Long Nose" pliers. It requires more delicacy than the Thompson "Duplex," but it will serve better after your touch has been established.

Hair Stacker

There is very little difference among stackers. All do the job well. Any edge would go to the Crest Hair Stacker because of price and quality of manufacture.

HOOKS

Anatomy of a Fly Tying Hook

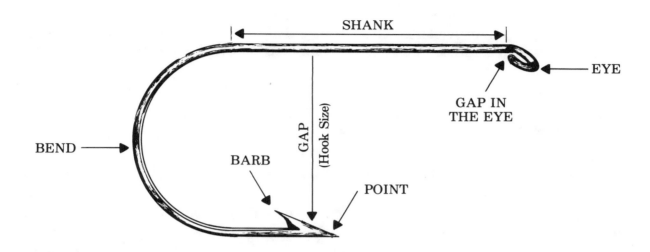

Standard Shank. The length is one and one-half time the width of the hook gap. As gap, or hook size, increases, the shank will increase proportionally in length.

Long Shank. This is a longer shank than a standard. A 1X long means that a 1X long hook shank is equal to a standard length shank, 1 hook size larger. Shank length of size 10, 1X long hook will equal length of size 8 standard shank. A 2X long refers to shank length equal to standard shank, 2 sizes larger; 3X, 3 sizes larger; 4X, 4 sizes larger.

Short Shank. The reverse of a long shank.

Weight of Hook. The weight of a hook is determined by the diameter of wire used in making the hook. Light or fine wire is smaller and lighter than standard or heavy wire. Fine wire is used for dry flies, and heavier wire is used for strength when weight is not important.

t.d. or t.u. eye. This stands for turned **down** or turned **up** eye.

tap. eye. This is an abbreviation for **tapered** eye. To achieve this effect, the wire is cut at an angle and looped back, so that junction of the wire at the eye will parallel the hook wire.

HOOKS

Common Hook Styles

The style number used in fly tying hooks are usually Mustad hook style numbers. Mustad hooks are manufactured in Norway and have become the hook accepted by most tyers as the best hook available. There are others that match or exceed Mustad's quality. V.M.C. hooks are an example. Mustad hook numbers are still the most widely used.

Mustad Style No.	Type of Hook
3906	Standard shank, standard wire—wet fly
3906B	1X long shank, standard wire—wet fly
9671	2X long shank, forged wire (light, but forged for strength)—nymph or wet fly
9672	3X long, standard wire—nymph, streamer, or wooly worm
38941	3X long, forged—streamer, nymph, or grasshopper
79580	4X long standard wire—wooly worm, long bodied nymph, or long bodied streamer
3665A	6X long, standard wire—extremely long bodied nymph or streamer
94840	Standard shank, light wire—dry fly
94842	Same as 94840 except turned up eye
94845	Same as 94840 except barbless
3257B	Same as 3906 except barbless

This is not a complete list of hook styles, but these styles are the most commonly used. Every author or pattern originator has his favorite hook which may or may not be included in this list. Common sense will be your guide when substituting your hooks for a proposed hook. It is impossible to have every hook style, in every size, in your inventory.

At this point I would like to "plug" barbless hooks. Fishing with either barbless hooks or hooks with barbs pinched down, will allow you to release fish unharmed to catch again another day. God's streams are a flower garden to be enjoyed by everyone. If each passer-by picks as many blossoms as he can, the next time he passes that way he will find no more blossoms. If each only picked one or a very few blossoms, while they are at their peak, the flowers will continue to proliferate, for all to enjoy.

KNOTS

Importance of Knots

In every endeavor or new hobby, there are some tedious bits of preparation you must master before the real fun can begin. Fly tying is no exception. A beginning tyer must learn how to start and how to finish a fly before tying the finished product.

By now, you are thinking, "I really don't want to start here—I'll skip to the good part." Before you skip this section, let me convince you that a few minutes spent studying the next several pages will greatly enhance the pleasures of tying, and you will truly be prepared to enjoy the process of tying your first fly.

Set up your vise, bobbin and thread, scissors, and dubbing needle. Put a size 8 hook in your vise, and invest a few minutes with knots.

I would like to make two points before you begin.

1. Relax. You may not have everything working for you the first time through. Do not worry. You will get it. Each time you go through the instructions, it will be easier and it will make more sense.
2. Positive Pressure on the thread is necessary in each step. I do not mean hard pressure. Use only enough tension on the thread to keep it snug.

Setting the Hook in the Vise

The *only* proper way to set the hook in the vise is illustrated in the following picture. Place the hook so that the bend is covered by the jaws of the vise. Do not set the hook so that the point or barb are inside the jaws. The point and barb are very fragile and can be damaged easily. The hook shank should be parallel with your table.

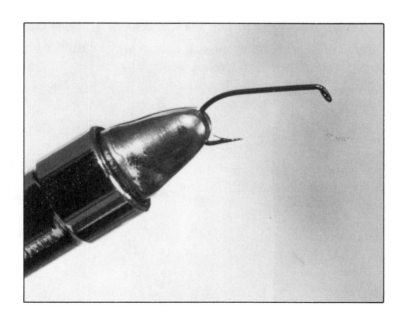

KNOTS

Attaching Thread to Hook

The first problem confronting a beginning fly tyer is how to attach the thread to the hook so that all other materials may be tied in and fixed to the hook. This is done by a simple "knot" called the jam knot. It really is not a knot but a process that traps the loose end of the thread to the hook shank with several wraps of thread extending from the bobbin. A jam knot is completed by following the steps listed below.

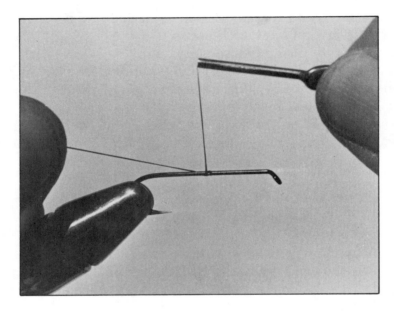

1. Hold bobbin in right hand above the hook and the loose thread in your left hand below the hook.*
2. Rest the thread against the side of the hook shank with positive pressure.
3. Hold your left hand in a stationary position and wrap bobbin and thread away from you around the hook with positive pressure.
4. Each wrap should be toward the bend of the hook, wrapping over the thread extending from your left hand.
5. Watch Out for the Hook Point!! As you wrap, see-saw the thread around the hook point.
6. After two wraps, angle the thread in your left hand gradually toward the bend until the thread is parallel with the hook shank after five or six wraps.

Attaching Thread to Hook cont.

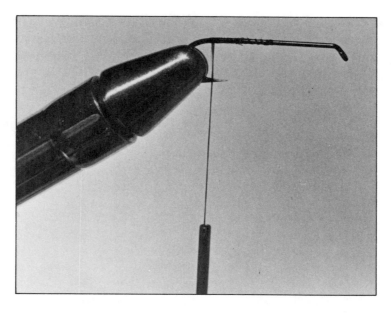

7. Let your bobbin hang. Your thread extending from the bobbin to the hook shank should be resting halfway between the hook point and the hook barb. This is the *starting position* for your thread when tying most flies.

8. Cut off the loose end of your thread.

*Instructions from here on are described for a right handed tyer. Left handed tyers must reverse directions, substituting left for right.

KNOTS

The Half Hitch

The half hitch is a simple knot used to hold the thread securely to the hook so that the tyer can release tension on the thread or bobbin and not lose what he has already wrapped. The illustration below shows the half hitch being tied step by step before it is pulled snug. To tie the half hitch, follow the steps listed below.

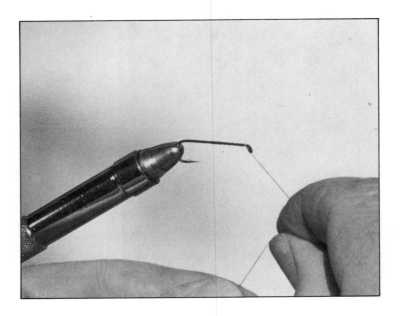

1. Pull out four to six inches of thread from the bobbin.
2. Hold the bobbin loosely in your left hand so that the spool rests in your palm, and your left thumb and forefinger are together at the top of the tube.
3. Grab the thread midway from bobbin to hook with your right thumb and forefinger, placing your thumb on the far side of the thread and your forefinger on the near side. DO NOT LET GO!!!

KNOTS

The Half Hitch cont.

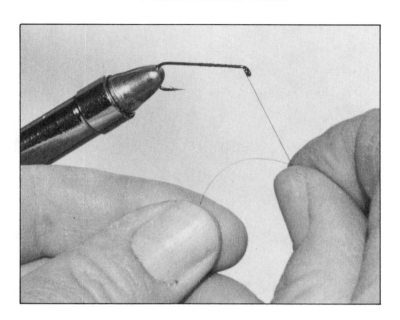

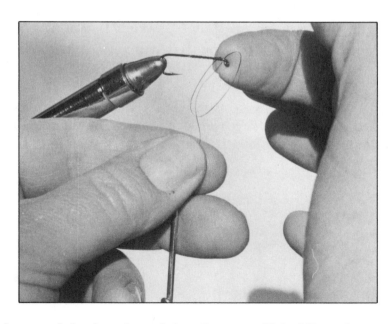

4. Reach up with your left thumb and forefinger, still holding the spool, and grab the thread an inch or so below the hook. When you reach up, reach *behind* your right fingers.

5. Place your right thumb and forefinger, while still holding the thread, behind the hook at the eye.

The Half Hitch cont.

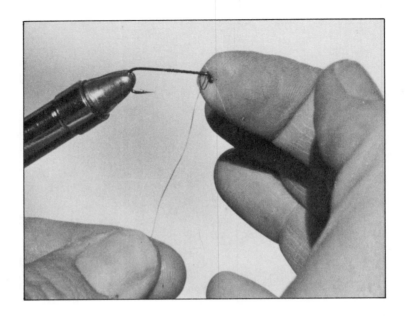

6. Move your right thumb and forefinger toward you, trapping the thread behind the hook with your right forefinger.
7. Press the thread against the hook with your right finger.
8. Release your right thumb, your left thumb, and left forefinger.
9. Now pull gently with the bobbin in your left hand and draw the loop in snug.

Note: While pulling the loop snug, your right thumb can be used to keep the loop in position to the right of the hook eye. This will keep control of the loop and place it exactly where you want it and prevent the loop from inadvertently catching hackles in the loop as it is tightened. ·

KNOTS

The Whip Finish

The whip finish is a knot used to finish a fly. This knot buries the end of the thread beneath four or five wraps. It ensures there are no loose ends and that the fly will remain intact while casting and fishing. The whip finish is so secure that head cement is unnecessary on most flies. To tie a whip finish, follow the steps listed below.

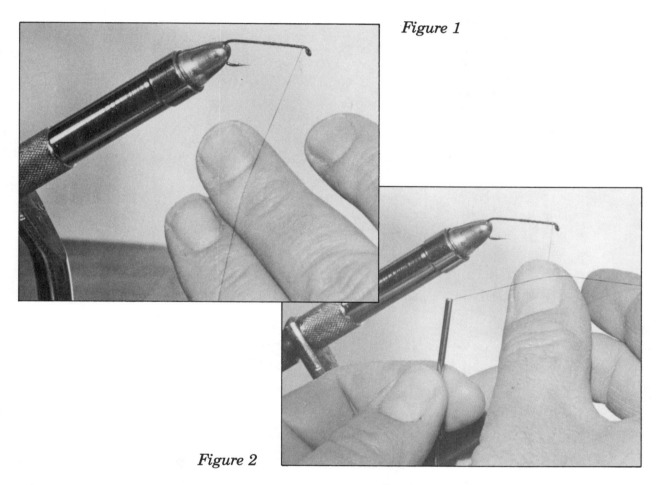

Figure 1

Figure 2

1. Half hitch immediately behind the eye.
2. Pull out 9 or 10 inches of thread.
3. Hold bobbin in left hand loosely so spool rests in palm, gripping loosely with little finger, while left thumb and forefinger are at the top of tube.
4. Place your right thumb, forefinger, and middle finger behind the thread, thumb pointed *down*, midway between the hook and the bobbin, so that the thread rests across the back of your first knuckle. (Figure 1)
5. Keep left hand below the hook with no tension on thread.
6. To make loop, roll your right hand so that palm faces you, thumb pointed *up*, keeping all three fingers, (forefinger, middle finger and thumb), inside the loop. (Figure 2)

KNOTS

The Whip Finish cont.

7. With your right thumb and forefinger, grab the thread extending from hook. DO NOT LET GO! (Figure 3)

8. Extend middle finger (still inside loop), expanding loop and guiding thread from bobbin to middle finger underneath and to opposite side of eye. (Figure 4)

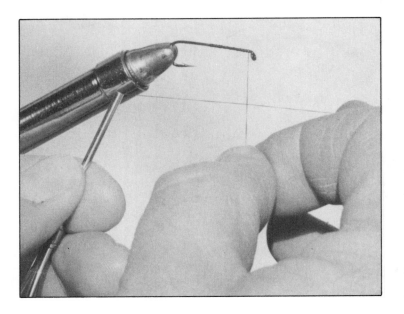

Figure 3

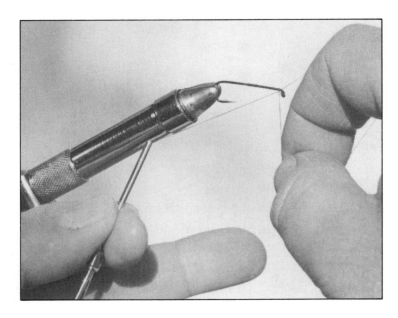

Figure 4

18

KNOTS

The Whip Finish cont.

9. Roll your right hand away from you, (roll your thumb from down to up position), pulling up with thread trapped between right thumb and forefinger above the hook and rotating middle finger away and down below hook. (Figure 5)

10. Raise your left thumb and forefinger to two inches below the hook to just in back of the eye.

11. Pull middle finger out of loop. Do not pull with left hand. *All* tension is applied by the right fingers.

12. Continue to wrap with your right thumb and forefinger around and down to meet your left thumb and forefinger.

13. Grab the thread with your left thumb and forefinger. (Figure 6)

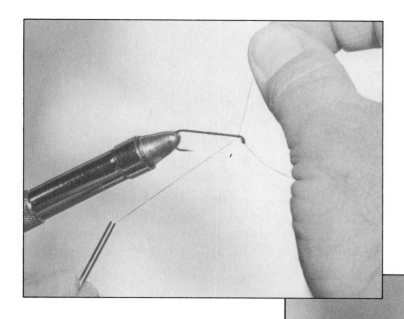

Figure 5

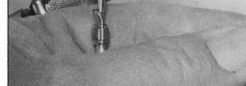

Figure 6

KNOTS

The Whip Finish cont.

14. Release right thumb and forefinger and bring them around the loop and regrab the thread held by your left fingers. (Figure 7)
15. Wrap another full wrap to your left fingers. Repeat step 14.
16. Repeat step 15 three or four more times.
17. Grab thread with your left thumb and forefinger. Put dubbing needle or scissors in loop with right hand. (Figure 8)
18. Maintain tension with tool, and gently draw loop in snug. (Figure 9)
19. Cut thread. The fly is now whip finished.

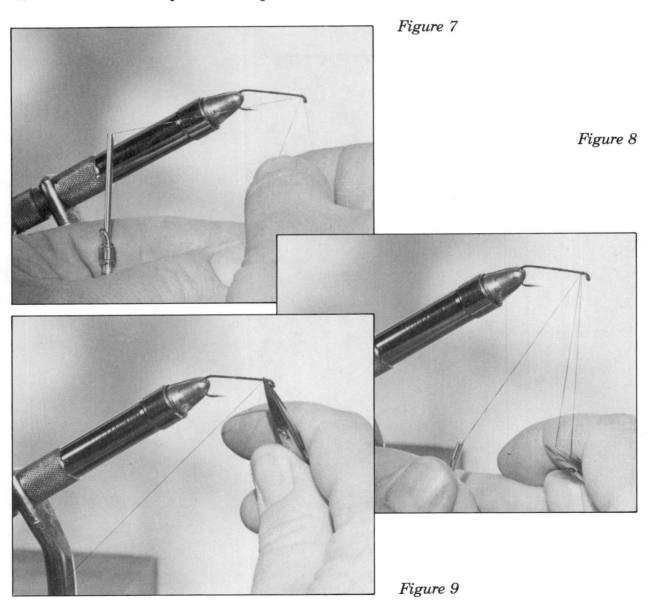

Figure 7

Figure 8

Figure 9

YOUR FIRST FLY

The Wooly Worm

After practicing your knots and learning how to start and finish a fly, you are ready for your first fly. The first fly is a simple, basic tie, but probably the one fly that counts for more trout than any other fly. It is also fished more than any other fly. The Wooly Worm does not *imitate* anything usually found in a trout's diet. It may appear to imitate a caterpillar, but when have you ever seen a caterpillar in a trout stream? On rare occasions, when conditions are just right, a caterpillar may invade the domain of the aquatic insect. The Wooly Worm may, instead, suggest to the trout a large variety of normally edible life from stone flies to leeches.

The Wooly Worm is tied with the following materials. The materials are listed in the order in which they are tied, or applied, to the hook. When the materials list is written in that order, it is called a dressing.

Hook: 79580
Head: Black
Tail: None
Body: Brown or black chenille
Hackle: Brown or black saddle hackle feather

To tie a Wooly Worm, follow the steps listed below.

1. Place hook in your vise.
2. Attach your thread, and wrap to normal starting position. (Point on hook shank halfway between point & barb.)

YOUR FIRST FLY

The Wooly Worm cont.

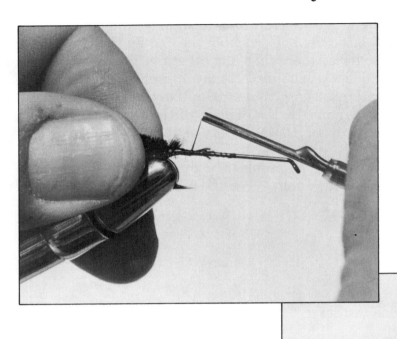

3. Cut a six to eight inch length of chenille, and prepare the chenille for attaching to the hook. The chenille is prepared by stripping the fuzz from it so that one-fourth to one-half inch of bare threads are exposed.

4. Hold the prepared chenille between your left thumb and forefinger with the bare threads extending to your right.

5. Place your left thumb and forefinger on top of the jaws of your vise, using the vise as a platform or brace, and tie in the chenille threads. This is best accomplished by wrapping loosely on the first wrap around the hook and increasing tension on the second, third, and fourth wraps. Each wrap should progress toward the bend of the hook. Continue to tie the chenille, wrapping your thread over the chenille to the point where the shank ends and the bend begins. Let your bobbin hang free.

The Wooly Worm cont.

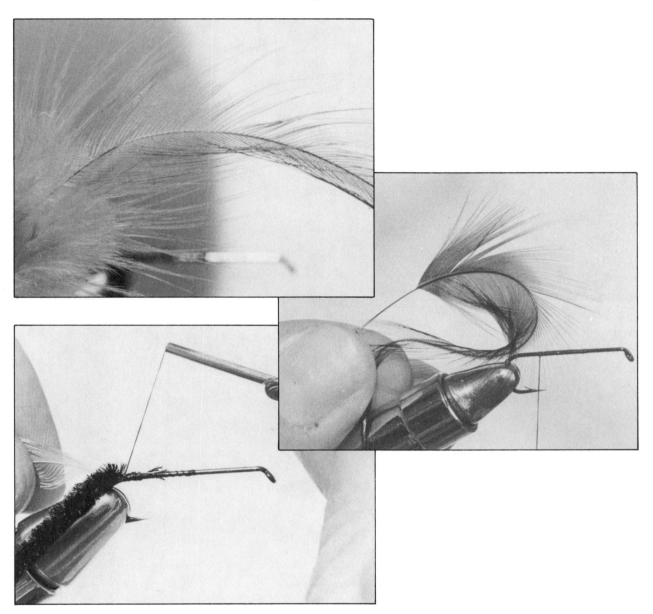

6. Select your saddle hackle. A saddle hackle feather suitable for tying a Wooly Worm will be three to five inches long and relatively even in width from the butt end of the feather to the tip.

7. Prepare feather as shown above. Strip fuzzy part and heavily webbed part of the feather from the quill with your thumbnail leaving the quill exposed.

8 . Tie in the feather as shown, starting your first wrap from where the thread is hanging, your last wrap on the chenille, and wrap toward the bend four or five times. Cut off excess butt, and wrap thread forward to the eye. Wraps need not be close.

YOUR FIRST FLY

The Wooly Worm cont.

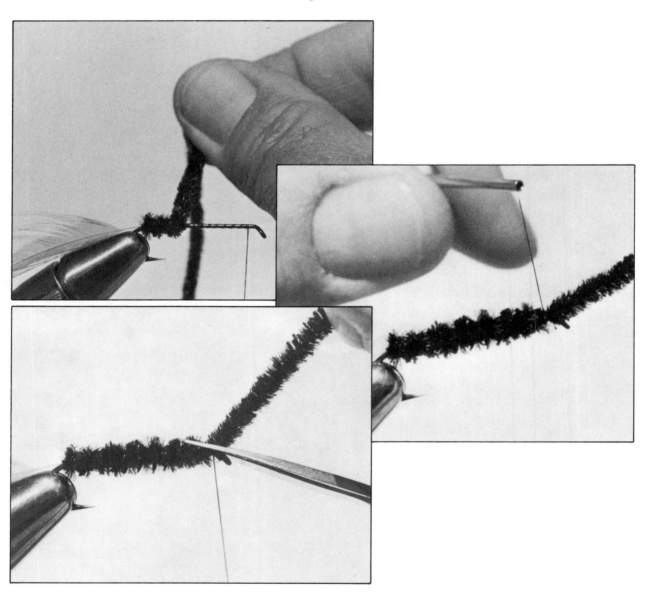

9. Wrap chenille, starting the first wrap where the shank ends and the bend starts. Continue to wrap the chenille, butting each wrap into the last, making an even, fat body.

10. Wrap all the way to the eye. Now, unwrap one full wrap. *Always* leave room at the eye to finish a head and whip finish the thread.

11. Hold the chenille in your right hand, pull it up and slightly to your right. Grab the bobbin in your left hand, wrap the thread around to the far side of the hook, (over the chenille), and drop the bobbin. Repeat this tying off process three times.

12. Cut excess chenille close to the hook. Always cut from the top. That will save cutting the thread which is hanging below the hook.

The Wooly Worm cont.

13. To wrap the feather, first reach under the vise and grab the feather gently at the tip with your left hand and wrap it under and toward you, placing the quill at the rear edge of the chenille body. Now, place the hackle pliers on the tip of the feather and continue to wrap spacing the wraps out so that the hackle is palmered (spacing hackle wraps with slight gap between) to the end of the body.

14. Tie off the hackle in the same manner you tied off the chenille in step 11, and cut excess tip.

15. Finish head by wrapping thread over loose butts of chenille and hackle, making a neat head. Do not make the head too big; only a few wraps are necessary.

16. Half hitch and whip finish.

YOUR FIRST FLY

Tying Tip #1

COVER THE ENTIRE SHANK OF THE HOOK

If your Wooly Worm, or any other pattern, does not extend from the start of the bend to just behind the eye, you are not tying in proportion to the hook size you have chosen. Obviously, a size 6 Wooly Worm should be larger than a size 8 or size 10. The body should be longer and the hackles should also be longer.

Additional Patterns*

1. **Brown Wooly Worm**
   Hook: 79580
   Thread: Black
   Body: Brown Chenille
   Hackle: Brown, Black or Grizzly Saddle Hackle

2. **Peacock Wooly Worm**
   Hook: 79580
   Thread: Black
   Body: Peacock Herl
   Hackle: Grizzly

3. **Yellow Wooly Worm**
   Hook: 79580
   Thread: Black
   Body: Yellow Chenille
   Hackle: Brown Saddle Hackle

4. **Olive Wooly Worm**
   Hook: 79580
   Thread: Black
   Body: Olive Chenille
   Hackle: Brown Saddle Hackle

5. **Grey Wooly Worm**
   Hook: 79580
   Thread: Black
   Body: Grey Chenille
   Hackle: Black or Grizzly

*If possible always have a color picture of a finished fly to refer to when tying a new or different pattern. A good source for color pictures are good quality mail order catalogues such as Orvis.

WET FLIES & NYMPHS

When my brother Dick and I were taught to Trout Fish on the Brazos & Chama Rivers in Northern New Mexico by a grand lady named Ruth Willy, we often used flies as well as bait. Many times we used flies only using a tail fly and a second fly on a dropper. When Mrs. Willy approached the stream and decided upon the terminal tackle for that day, if it were flies, the decision was made to fish a fly either wet or dry. If the decision was "dry" the fly was dressed with Muscilin and floated. If the decision was "wet" the same fly was tied on, dropped in the mud, and stepped on. I fished for years without knowing there was a difference between wet and dry flies.

One question I am asked more than any other today is "what is the difference between a dry fly and a wet fly?" The obvious answer is the dry fly floats and the wet fly sinks. Too simple? — probably but it still is true. To really understand the difference I have to take you with me to the bottom of a stream to watch and understand the life cycle of some of the insects we attempt to suggest or imitate with furs and feathers attached to a hook.

Beginning as an egg on the bottom of a stream, a May Fly nymph takes form and grows, taking up to a year (or even longer in some cases) to develop and mature. Finally, the time is right for the metamorphosis from aquatic nymph to airbourne adult. The nymph must travel somehow from the bottom of the stream to the surface. Some nymphs swim; some even bob up and down in the current gathering air bubbles in fine filament-like gill structures. They become more and more bouyant until they float to the surface. On the way to the surface the adult May Fly begins to emerge. The nymph case splits lengthwise over the thorax and the wings of the adult unfold, streaming back. The adult's head and legs emerge from the case and the nymph begins to look more like the adult form of the May Fly. Finally the emerging stage of the nymph, or emerger, reaches the surface and the adult crawls through the surface film to sit on top of the water. The adult unfolds the wings and extends them straight up to dry. These fine fragile wings must be dry before the May Fly can become airbourne.

As you visualize these steps in the life cycle of an insect two things become obvious. At each stage, the nymph beginning the migration from bottom to surface, the emerging insect, and the adult waiting for wings to dry, is extremely visable and vulnerable. A great food source for Trout. The "hatch" that is so much a part of fly fishing lore, is Mother Nature's way of ringing the dinner bell for Trout.

The second obvious point is the different appearance of each of these three stages of the insect. The nymph is all legs and body with no obvious wings. The emerger, our wet fly, is less body and legs with obvious wings *not* upright but streaming over the back, and relatively low in profile. The dry fly, or adult stage, is small in body, with distinct tail and legs and the most predominant feature, the wings, being large and upright.

As you look at a fly don't try to view it as an imitation of a specific insect, but rather as a caricature of that stage of an insect. A caricature that takes a predominent feature and emphasizes that feature.

The Montana Nymph

The Montana Nymph has become one of the most popular patterns to imitate the nymph stage of the stone fly. Most stone flies live on stream bottoms. The nymph must crawl out of the water, either on a rock, limb, or even the bank, to hatch into an adult. Therefore, this nymph only occurs deep in the stream and must be fished deep to be effective. "Salmon fly" or "Willow fly" are other names used to describe a Stone fly in different parts of the country.

A fishing friend of mine, who graciously read my first text for errors, David Poole, would fish a Montana Nymph in a Midge hatch.

The Montana Nymph is tied with the following materials:

Hook: Mustad 79580
Head: Black
Tail: Black feather barbules
Abdomen: Black chenille
Thorax: Yellow chenille
Hackle: Black saddle palmered over thorax
Wing Case: Black chenille

To tie a Montana Nymph, follow the steps listed below.

1. Set hook in the vise and start your thread. (This is the last time I will include this step since it is obvious to every pattern.)
2. Select a saddle hackle feather. The feather you should look for is three to five inches long and more spade-shaped than the long, narrow hackle feather you selected for the Wooly Worm.

The Montana Nymph cont.

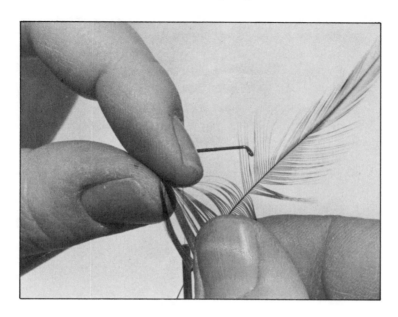

3. The tail will come from the bottom of the hackle. Save the top part. You will use it for the hackle over the thorax.

4. Grab the feather tip in your right hand and with your left thumb and forefinger gently pull the barbules (the fibres attached to the center quill) down toward the butt of the feather. Pull them down several times until the barbules stand out at a 90 degree angle to the quill. Pull off the fuzz at the base of the feather, so it will be out of your way.

5. Holding the right side of the feather in your right hand at a right angle to your left thumb and forefinger, place the ends of the barbules on the left side between your left finger tips. Close your left thumb and forefinger tip, trapping as many barbule ends as you can firmly between your finger tips. Grap the feather at the top with your right hand and pull the feather down and away from your left finger tips, separating the barbules from the quill.

6. Do not let go with your left thumb and forefinger!

The Montana Nymph cont.

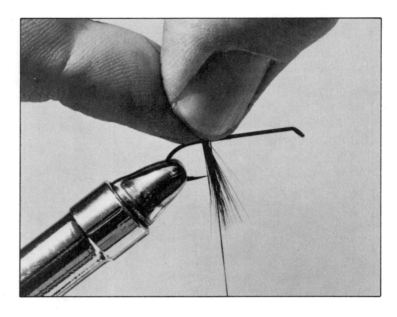

7. Take the butts of the tail barbules in your right thumb and forefinger. Now let go with your left fingers. Your tail should look like a small paint brush.

8. With your right fingers still holding the tail, size the tail by holding the tips down over the hook shank past the hook point. The length of the tail should be one and one-half times to two times the hook gap.

9. When the tail is sized, take the sized tail length between your left thumb and forefinger. Everything now trapped between your finger tips is that part of the tail that will extend from the hook shank.

10. Set your left thumb and forefinger on top of the vise with the butts of the tail extending over the hook shank toward the eye. The tail trapped in your left fingers will extend from the point on the shank just before the bend starts.

Note: *I cannot emphasize this tailing technique enough! It is critical when tying dry flies.*

The Montana Nymph cont.

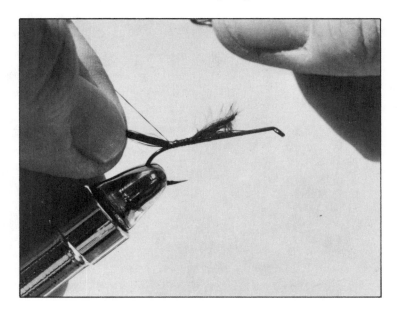

11. Tie in the tail. Make the first wrap loose. After the second wrap, while still holding the tail in your left fingers, pull up slightly on the tail to angle the tail up off the top of the hook shank.

12. Continue to hold the tail up and wrap the thread toward the bend. As your wraps progress, drop the tail until at the last wrap, (make last wrap almost loose), the tail is held level with the shank. Continue to hold the tail, and take two wraps toward the eye.

13. Now, you can let go with your left fingers. Your tail should be on top of the shank extending straight back. Carefully clip the excess butts off the tail.

The Montana Nymph cont.

14. Prepare the black chenille and tie in just as you did in the Wooly Worm. Wrap the thread back over the chenille to the start of the bend (where your tail comes off the shank). Do not go too far or the tail will be ruined.

15. Advance the thread half way up the shank toward the eye. Wrap the black chenille to the thread and tie off. Be sure that you tie off from the top and have the black chenille coming straight up off the shank.

16. Do *not* cut your black chenille, but lay it back over the vise, out of your way.

The Montana Nymph cont.

17. Tie in the yellow chenille directly in front of the black.

18. Tie in the black saddle you used for tail material. First strip the bottom webby barbules and use only the top part of the feather. Wrap the thread to just behind the eye, and close the gap.

19. Wrap the yellow chenille to behind the eye and back up one full wrap. Leave a lot of room at the eye. Tie off yellow chenille and clip.

20. Palmer the black hackle over the yellow chenille to the forward edge of the yellow chenille and tie off the hackle. Clip the excess hackle tip.

The Montana Nymph cont.

21. With your scissors, carefully clip all of the hackle from the top of the thorax (yellow chenille). Do not clip too close. Be sure not to clip your black chenille.

22. Pull black chenille over the thorax past the eye and in line with the shank. Tie off carefully so that the wing case does not roll away from you. Do not pull the chenille tight, but lay it loose so that thread wraps will be snug. Tie off and clip excess black chenille carefully, so that you do not cut your thread. Take two more wraps with your thread, tying slightly back toward the thorax, to make sure that the wing case is securely tied.

23. Finish head covering loose ends. Half hitch and whip finish.

WET FLIES & NYMPHS

Tying Tip #2

MAKE EACH PART OF THE FLY DISTINCT

Since the Montana Nymph is a complex pattern, control of the materials is essential. Each part of the fly should be distinct. Your fly should have a distinct tail, abdomen, thorax, wing case, hackle, and head.

Additional Patterns

1. **Teds Stonefly**
   Hook: 79580
   Thread: Black
   Tail: Goose Quill Fibres
   Abdomen: Brown Chenille
   Wing Case: Brown Chenille
   Hackle: Black Saddle Hackle
   Thorax: Yellow Chenille

2. **Orange Montana Nymph**
   Hook: 79580
   Thread: Black
   Tail: Brown
   Abdomen: Black Chenille
   Wing Case: Black Chenille
   Hackle: Brown Saddle Hackle—palmered over Thorax
   Thorax: Orange Chenille

3. **Black Wooly Booger**
   Hook: 79580
   Thread: Black
   Tail: Black Maribou (or fluff from base of hackle)
   Body: Black Chenille
   Hackle: Black Saddle, palmered over length of body Wooly Worm style

4. **Olive Wooly Booger**
   Hook: 79580
   Thread: Black
   Tail: Black or Olive Maribou (or fluff form base of hackle)
   Body: Olive Chenille
   Hackle: Black or Olive Saddle, palmered over length of body Wooly Worm style

WET FLIES & NYMPHS

The Peacock Nymph

I am not sure where the Peacock Nymph originated. It may even have some old origins with other fore and aft flies: however, it has been enthusiastically adopted by New Mexico and Colorado fishermen. The Peacock Nymph will rival the Wooly Worm as the most fished fly in this two-state area.

When used in lakes or stiller waters, this fly suggests a dragon fly or damsel fly nymph. In faster flowing waters it may suggest a varity of trout food since it presents the same appearance from either end, making it appealing at dead drift or tighter line retrieve.

The Peacock Nymph is tied with the following materials:

Hook: Mustad 79580
Head: Black
Tail: None
Aft Hackle: Brown saddle or Brown neck
Body: Peacock herl
Fore Hackle: Brown saddle or Brown neck

To tie the Peacock Nymph, follow the steps listed below.

1. Select a hackle feather from a brown neck or brown saddle hackle. Gently separate the feather from the others and bend it as shown above to determine length of the barbules. Once a feather of the correct length has been found, pull it from the neck.

Prepare the brown neck hackle feather.

Note: *Barbule length should be approximately one and one-half to two times hook gap.*

The Peacock Nymph cont.

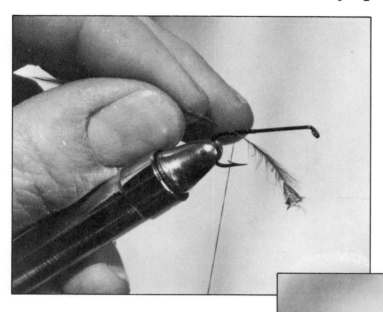

2. Tie in the hackle; tying in the bare quill with the butt toward the eye. Wrap thread back from the starting position toward the bend, making your last wrap at the end of the shank. Then wrap the thread forward, toward the eye, until you are at mid shank. This thread position does not represent the next tie-off place but only serves to move your thread out of your way.

3. Wrap hackle in standard wet fly style. A standard hackle wrap means that the feather is wrapped in virtually one spot on the shank, butting each wrap right in front of the previous one. Hackle wrap should cover as small a space on the hook shank as possible. Four to five wraps should be sufficient to give you a nice fluffy hackle.

4. Tie off hackle and cut excess. To do this, you will have to bring the thread back to position to tie off.

The Peacock Nymph cont.

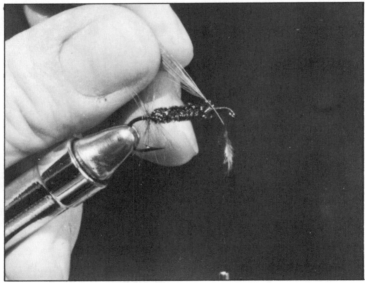

5. Select four or five peacock herls and even the tips. Tie in the tips and continue to tie back until your last thread wrap butts into the aft hackle. Cut off excess tips and advance thread to behind the eye.

6. Wrap strands of herl forward, overwrapping if necessary, to make a fat, fuzzy herl body. Tie off behind the eye, leaving plenty of room for another hackle to be wrapped and a finished head.

7. Prepare the fore hackle. Tie in and wrap just as you did for the aft hackle. Tie off and cut excess.

8. Finish head, half hitch, and whip finish.

WET FLIES & NYMPHS

Tying Tip #3

CONCENTRATE ON BALANCE AND SYMMETRY

No part of a fly should overpower the balance of the fly. Each part is distinct and important, but care should be taken to produce a finished fly that appears balanced.

Additional Patterns

1. **Renegade**
   Hook: 79580 or 9672
   Thread: Black
   Aft Hackle: Brown Saddle
   Body: Peacock
   Fore Hackle: White or Cream Saddle

2. **Warden's Worry***
   Hook: 79580 or 9672
   Thread: Black
   Aft Hackle: Grizzly Saddle**
   Body: Peacock Herl
   Fore Hackle: Brown Saddle**

3. **Double Renegade**
   Hook: 79580 or 9672
   Thread: Black
   Tail: Red Feather Barbule
   Aft Hackle: Brown Saddle
   Body: Peacock Herl
   Mid Hackle: White or Cream Saddle
   Fore Hackle: Brown Saddle

4. **Burlap Nymph**
   Hook: 79580 or 9672
   Thread: Black
   Aft Hackle: Brown Saddle
   Body: Burlap String or Twine (1 strand from burlap sack)
   Fore Hackle: Brown Saddle

*John Ferguson's favorite fly and one of my occasional fishing partners, Doug With, would give up all flies in his vest before he would let go of his Wardens Worry. Both use it to out fish me.

**many tyers prefer the reverse—Grizzly Fore & Brown Aft

WET FLIES & NYMPHS

The Grey Hackle Peacock

My introduction to fly fishing began with the Grey Hackle Peacock. It was good enough to convert me to fly fishing, and it still is a great fly for me. This pattern can be tied wet or dry. For our purposes, we will tie this pattern wet, and I heartily recommend it as another must for your fly box.

The Grey Hackle Peacock is tied with the following materials:

Hook: Mustad 3906B
Head: Black
Tail: Golden pheasant tippet fibres
Body: Peacock herl
Hackle: Grizzly neck

To tie the Grey Hackle Peacock, follow the steps listed below.

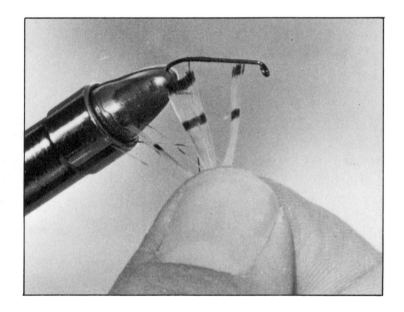

1. Select golden pheasant tippet feathers. Separate five or six fibres (or barbules) from the quill. Do not try to pull these off, but keeping the black bars even on the fibres, cut them off with scissors close to the quill.

The Grey Hackle Peacock cont.

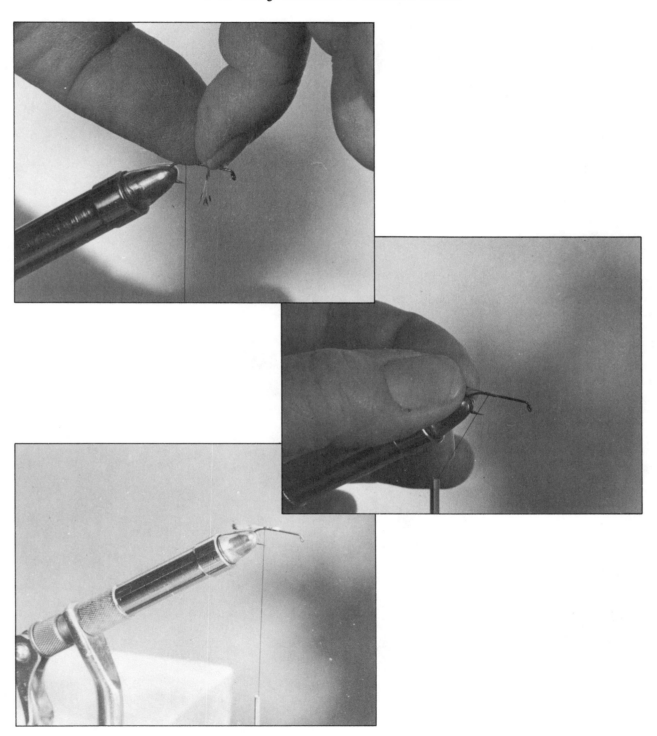

2. Size your tail, one and one-half to two times the gap, and tie in as you did in the Montana Nymph. Be sure that the black bars are even when tied in.

The Grey Hackle Peacock cont.

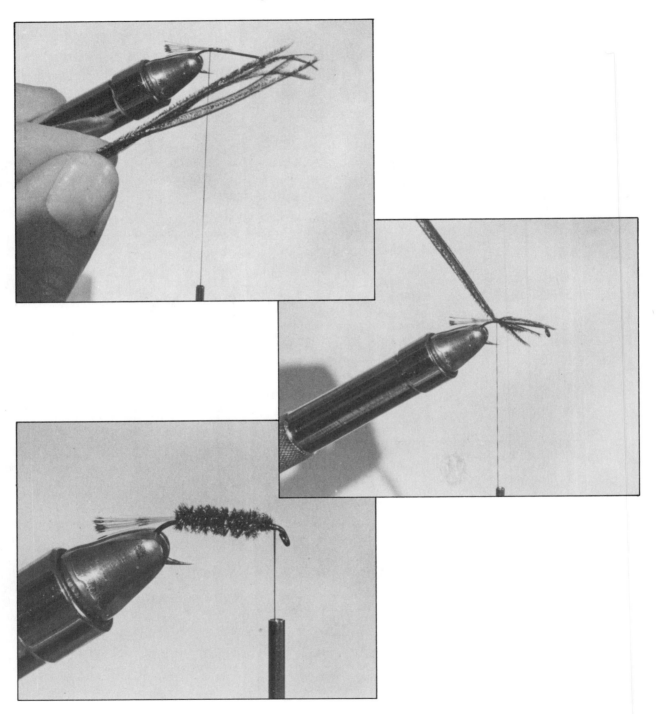

3. Select and tie in four to six peacock herls, and advance the thread to behind the eye.
4. Wrap peacock herl to behind the eye. Leave room; you have to provide for hackle and head. Tie off peacock herl, and cut excess butts.

The Grey Hackle Peacock cont.

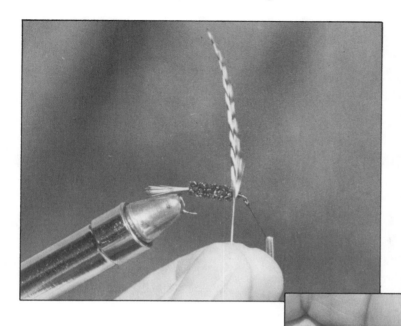

5. Select and prepare the right size hackle feather. Remember, barbules should be one and one-half to two times the hook gap.
6. Tie in the hackle feather wet fly style.

Note: *Every hackle feather has a natural curve. As you look at a feather, it will curve slightly from butt to tip. The direction of this curve, as it is tied in and wrapped onto the shank, will determine whether the hackle is wet or dry style. For a wet style hackle, the feather is tied in and wrapped so that the curve (or concave side) is toward the bend of the hook. Dry fly style is the opposite, with the curve toward the eye of the hook.*

The Grey Hackle Peacock cont.

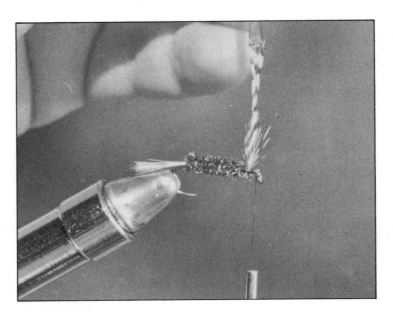

7. The easiest way to tie in a hackle, either wet or dry, is to determine the curve and place the feather on the hook shank at the point of tie-in at a 45 degree angle to the shank, with the tip toward the bend of the hook. For wet fly style, the concave side of the feather faces the bend of the hook.

8. Wrap hackle making sure that the first wrap of your hackle is at the forward edge of your body. Keep hackle on edge as you wrap, placing each wrap directly in front of the last wrap.

9. Tie off hackle, make neat head, half hitch, and whip finish.

WET FLIES & NYMPHS

Tying Tip #4

SOFT HACKLE IS BEST FOR WET FLIES

Too much emphasis is placed on stiff, high-quality neck hackle for dry flies, while the softer hackles are forgotten. The softer hackles flowing back toward the bend of the hook will give your wet fly life and movement in the water.

Additional Patterns

1. **Brown Hackle Peacock**
   Hook: 3906 or 3906B
   Thread: Black
   Tail: Red Hackle Barbules (Saddle)
   Body: Peacock Herl
   Hackle: Brown Saddle or Neck

2. **Black Hackle Red**
   Hook: 3906 or 3906B
   Thread: Black
   Tail: Red Barbules (Saddle Hackle)
   Body: Peacock Herl
   Hackle: Black (either Neck or Saddle)

3. **Breadcrust**
   Hook: 3906 or 3906B
   Thread: Black
   Tail: None
   Body: Brown Hackle Quill (see "Mosquito" page 71)
   Hackle: Grizzly

4. **Brown Hackle Red**
   Hook: 3906 or 3906B
   Thread: Black
   Tail: Red Barbule
   Body: Red Floss
   Hackle: Brown Neck or Saddle

WET FLIES & NYMPHS

The Rio Grande King

The Rio Grande King is an excellent example of a fly that is a caricature of a natural insect. Predominent features are emphasized to provide instant association to the real thing. In this case the wing is emphasized. An emerging May fly may often have the wing out of the nymph case, and the wing appears to dominate the fly.

The Rio Grande King is tied with the following materials:

Hook: Mustad 3906B
Head: Black
Tail: Golden Pheasant Tippet
Body: Black chenille
Wing: White duck quill
Hackle: Brown feather barbules—tied beard style

To tie the Rio Grande King, follow the steps listed below.

1. Size and apply the tail just as you did on the Grey Hackle Peacock.
2. Attach black chenille and advance your thread to behind eye.
3. Wind chenille body to the eye and back up at least one full wrap. Tie off chenille and cut excess chenille.
4. Make sure that you have a lot of room between the end of your chenille body and the eye.

The Rio Grande King cont.

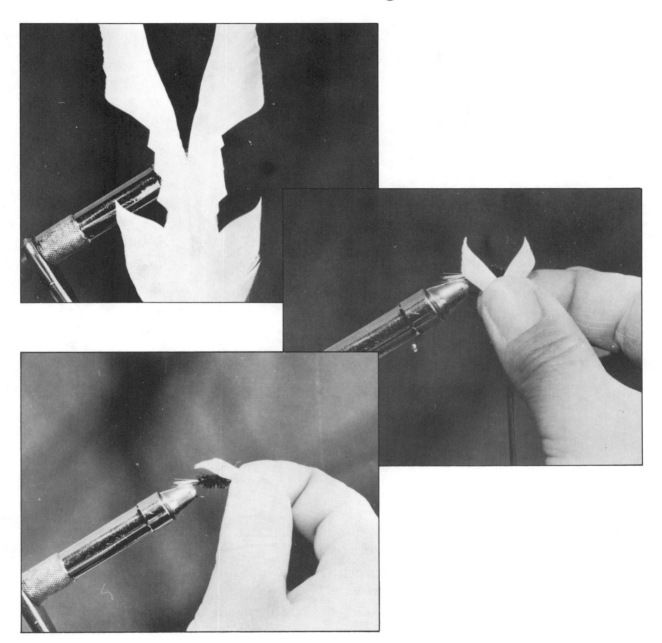

5. From a matched pair of wing quills (one right and one left) cut a small section from each quill. Notice that the feathers curve slightly. Set the quill sections together so that the tips are even and the curves oppose one another. In other words, set the quill sections so that the concave sides are together. Worry *only* that the tips, not the butts, are even. If the quill sections are different widths, gently remove excess quill to make each section about the width of the hook gap.

6. Set the wings on top of the hook and size them. The wing should curve down and extend slightly past the body.

The Rio Grande King cont.

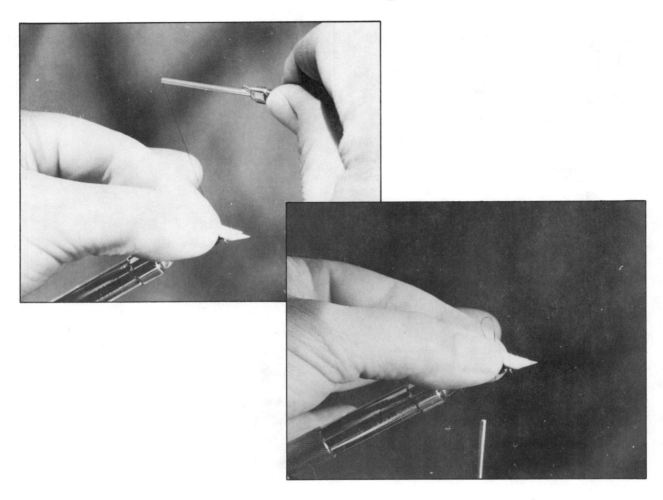

7. Grab the wings tightly between your left thumb and forefinger. All that is now buried between your fingertips is wing. All quill extending is either tied or cut off. Your thread should be directly in front of the chenille body.

8. Place your finger tips on the top of the hook shank with the front junction of your finger tips directly above your thread.

9. Pull up on the thread, trapping the thread between your thumb and the wing. Take thread over and down, trapping it between your forefinger tip and the wing. Leave a loop on top.

10. Gently pull the loop snug to the top of the wing. *Do not* pull tight.

11. Repeat steps 9 and 10.

12. While holding left thumb and forefinger tips tight on wings pull straight down with bobbin, crushing wing quills to the top of the shank. Do not let go with your left finger tips.

13. Take two or three wraps toward the eye.

The Rio Grande King cont.

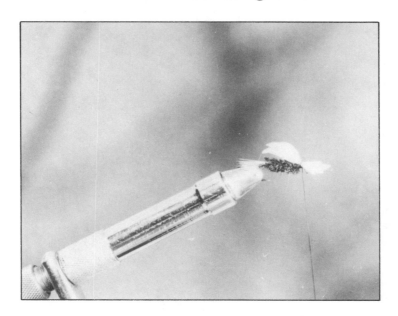

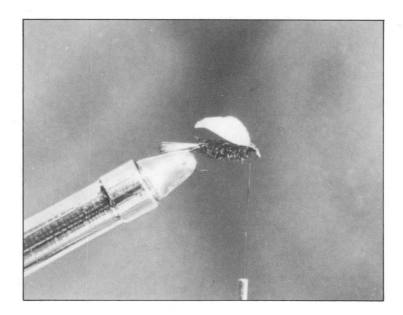

14. Now let go of your wing. It should be on top of the shank and not rolled. If it has rolled, it means that you did not hold the wing tight enough or pull down straight and hard when tying in the wing.

15. *Carefully* clip excess butts, and take two or three more wraps to cover the wing butts.

The Rio Grande King cont.

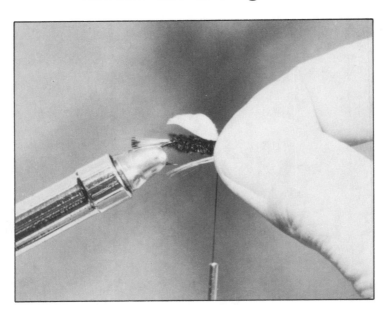

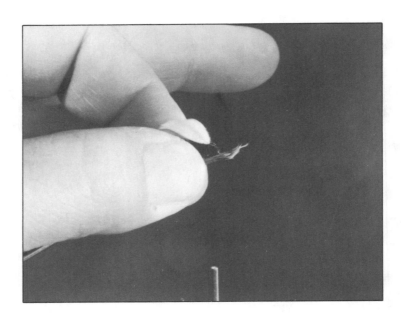

16. Take a feather from the top of your neck. Strip the barbules as your did for the Montana Nymph Tail.

17. Size them by holding them in your right fingers and setting the bunch just below the eye with tips extending past the hook point. When sized, reach from behind the vise with thumb and forefinger of left hand to grap the barbule bunch under the hook.

18. Tie in beard, taking care to keep under the hook shank. Clip excess, finish head, half hitch, and whip finish.

WET FLIES & NYMPHS

Tying Tip #5

CONTROL OF MATERIALS

Quill wings are *not* easy to tie. Many tyers do not even attempt the use of quills and instead use calf tail or other substitutes.

A few minutes' practice with a bare hook and quill wings will give you a feel for tying quills wings consistently and correctly. Do not let the materials control you. Decide that you can and will control the materials.

Additional Patterns

1. **Leadwing Coachman**
   Hook: 3906 or 3906B
   Thread: Black
   Tail: None
   Tag: Gold Tinsel (2 or 3 tinsel wraps where bend of the hook meets shank)
   Body: Peacock Herl
   Wing: Grey Wing Quill
   Hackle: Brown Neck or Saddle

2. **Black Gnat**
   Hook: 3906 or 3906B
   Thread: Black
   Tail: Black Barbules
   Body: Black Chenille
   Wing: Grey Wing Quill
   Hackle: Black Neck or Saddle

3. **Coachman**
   Hook: 3906 or 3906B
   Thread: Black
   Tail: None
   Tag: Gold Tinsel (2 or 3 tinsel wraps where bend of the hook meets shank).
   Body: Peacock Herl
   Wing: White Duck Quill (or White Deer Body Hair).
   Hackle: Brown Neck or Saddle

4. **Alder**
   Hook: 3906 or 3906B
   Thread: Black
   Tag: Gold Tinsel
   Body: Peacock Herl
   Wing: Mottled Turkey Wing
   Hackle: Black Neck or Saddle

WET FLIES & NYMPHS

The Muskrat Nymph

A good, simple nymph pattern is essential for a complete fly box. Every fly fisherman needs a plain vanilla pattern to fish when the exotic and imitative patterns are not producing or do not feel right. I have adopted the Muskrat Nymph as my general purpose nymph.

The Muskrat Nymph is tied with the following materials.

Hook: Mustad 9671
Head: Black
Tail: None
Weight: Lead wire
Body: Dubbed muskrat fur
Hackle: Grizzly neck

To tie the Muskrat Nymph, follow the steps listed below.

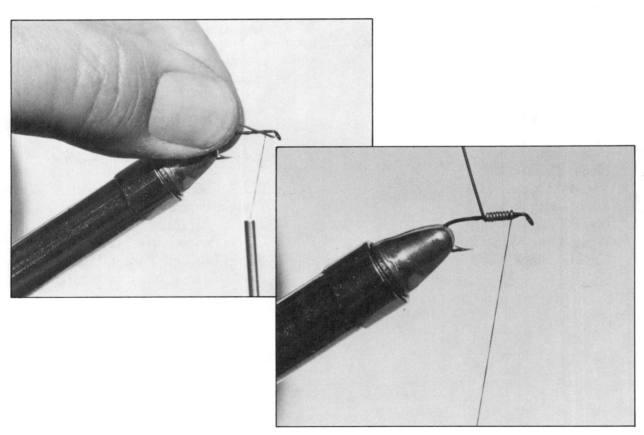

1. Start thread and wrap to just behind the eye.
2. Tie in a length of lead wire two to three inches long, one-eighth of an inch behind the eye. Wrap lead wire back toward the bend. Midway back on the shank, tie off the lead wire by wrapping thread back over lead wire and tie off.

The Muskrat Nymph cont.

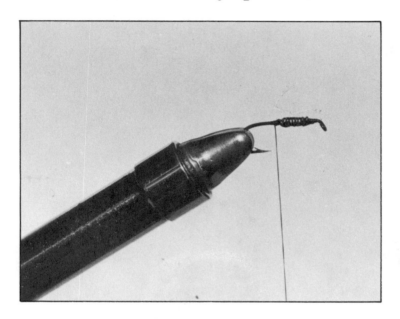

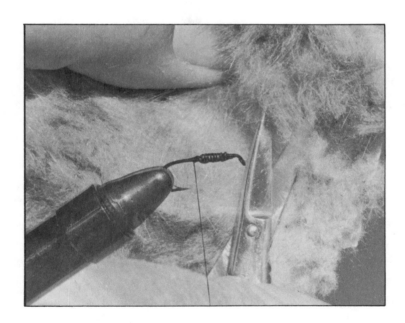

3. Clip off excess lead wire and wrap thread back and forth over lead wire making an even underbody. Bring thread back to starting position.

4. Cut a small amount of fur from your muskrat hide. Clip the fur close to the skin so that the clump of fur includes the soft underfur as well as the longer, stiffer guard hairs.

The Muskrat Nymph cont.

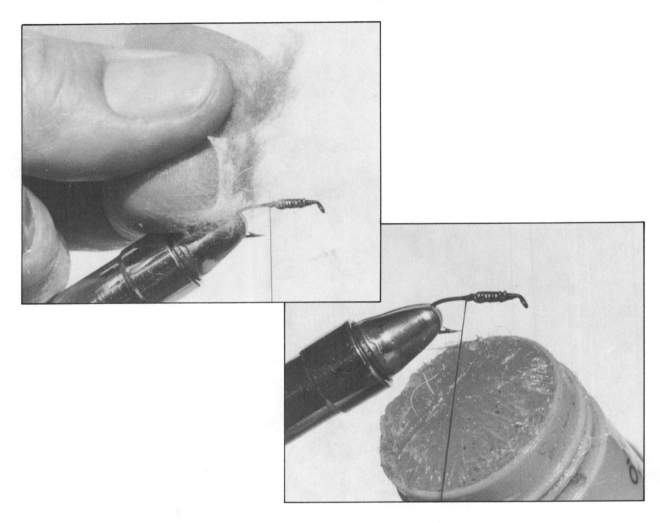

5. Gently pull the fur bunch between your left and right thumb and forefinger tips. Fold back together and pull apart, like pulling taffy, until a thin mat of fur is produced.

6. This mat should be long and narrow in shape.

7. Place this thin narrow mat to one side and select a proper size grizzly hackle. Prepare the hackle feather and tie it in at the bend of the hook.

8. Even though you are using a pre-waxed thread, a tackier wax must now be applied to your thread to help hold the fur to the thread. Apply a light coat of dubbing wax to a three-inch length of thread from your hook shank to the top of your bobbin. Pull out another inch or so of thread from your bobbin.

Note: *A general rule of dubbing—take only the amount of fur you think necessary, take half of that, then take half of the remainder.*

The Muskrat Nymph cont.

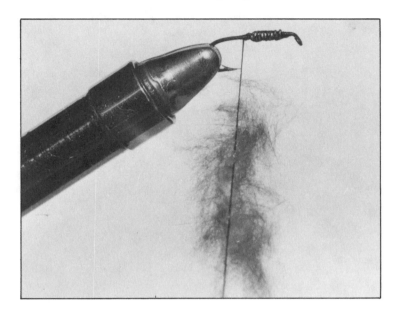

9. Gently take the mat of fur you have prepared and while holding the bobbin in your left hand, lightly place the fur mat against the back side of the thread so that the mat sticks to the thread.

10. Starting at the top of your fur mat, gently roll the fur between your right thumb and forefinger, forming a loose, fuzzy, round yarn of fur. Gradually work down toward the bobbin, being careful not to pull down since this will separate the fur mat.

11. Starting at the top again, roll the fur with a bit more pressure to form a tight yarn and continue rolling down the thread toward the bobbin.

The Muskrat Nymph cont.

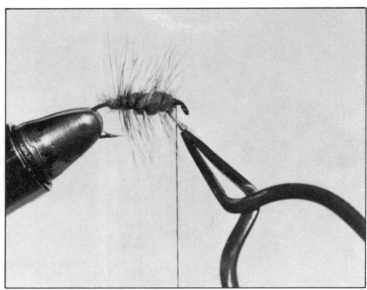

12. When you have formed a relatively tight yarn, begin to wrap the yarn by wrapping bobbin forward to just behind the eye. You can control the size of your body by over-wrapping, if necessary, and ending the wrap just behind the eye.

13. Tie off the dubbing. If you have an excess amount of fur, tie this off just as you would any other material. Tie three or four wraps back into the dubbing to ensure that it is tied securely to the hook.

14. Palmer your grizzly hackle forward, making the wraps fairly close to the end of the dubbed body. Tie off the hackle and cut the excess. Half hitch and whip finish.

Tying Tip #6

HACKLE GUARDS

There are times when it would be extremely helpful to have the hackle pulled back, away from the eye to allow a neat whip finish. Commercial hackle guards are awkward and generally not satisfactory. Try a section of drinking straw one-half inch long and slit along the side. Slide the thread through the slit and position the straw over your hackle. When finished, just pull it off.

Additional Patterns

1. **Brown Nymph**
   Hook: 3906B
   Thread: Black
   Tail: None
   Body: Dubbed Brown Fur
   Wing Case: Pheasant Tail Fibres (See Wing Case instructions for Gold Ribbed Hare's Ear)
   Hackle: Brown

2. **Black Ant**
   Hook: 94840
   Thread: Black
   Tail: None
   Wings: None
   Body: rear half—dubbed ball of Black Fur or Poly—front half—same.
   Hackle: Black or Brown wrapped between body segments (sparse)

3. **Dark Hendrickson**
   Hook: 3906B
   Thread: Black
   Tail: Dyed Woodduck or Mallard Side
   Rib: Brown Floss
   Abdomen: Grey Dubbed Fur
   Wing Case: Turkey Quill Segment
   Thorax: Grey Dubbed Fur—larger than abdomen
   Hackle: Brown Barbules tied beard style

4. **Colorado Caddis**
   Hook: 3906B
   Thread: Black
   Tail: None
   Body: Yellow Dubbed Fur
   Covert (wing case): Grey Duck or Goose Quill over entire body & hackle
   Hackle: Black

WET FLIES & NYMPHS

The Gold Ribbed Hare's Ear

If there was ever a nymph popularity contest, I think the Gold Ribbed Hare's Ear would easily win. Of all the hundreds of nymph patterns, this one is probably the most widely known and fished.

The general shape and hairy features make this nymph a classic in every sense. It may appear as either a large May fly nymph, a Caddis larvae, or a small Stone Fly nymph. The combination of ribbing and hare's ear furnish a texture and flash that seem to make it extremely attractive to trout.

The Gold Ribbed Hare's Ear is tied with the following materials:

Hook: Mustad 9671
Head: Black
Tail: Tuft of hair from mask or base of hare's ear
Abdomen: Dark, gold tipped hair from the ear.
Ribbing: Fine gold mylar tinsel
Thorax: Dark, gold tipped hair from the ear
Wing Case: Mottled turkey wing

To tie the Gold Ribbed Hare's Ear, follow the steps listed below.

1. Cut a small tuft of hair from the base of the hare's ear or mask. Hold this tuft at the tip of your left thumb and forefinger while gently fluffing the butt ends with your right fingertips to get rid of fine fur and short ends.

The Gold Ribbed Hare's Ear cont.

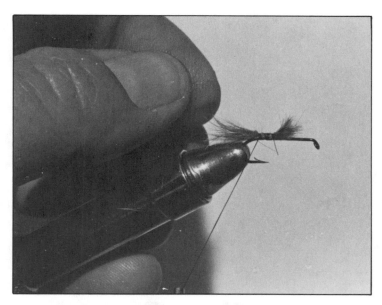

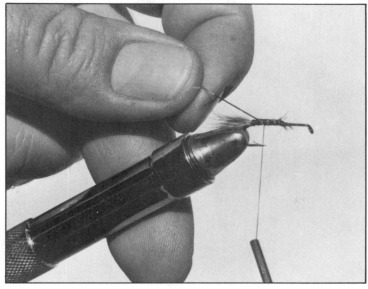

2. Tie in tail, making sure that it come straight off the top of the shank.
3. Tie in fine mylar tinsel with the silver side up.
4. You are now going to dub the abdomen using a different technique than the Muskrat Nymph.
5. Clip hair from the ear of the hare. Make a number of clips with your scissors as close to the skin as you can. Gather the clipped hairs by plucking them as you would a bird.
6. Prepare this mat just as you did in the Muskrat Nymph. Caution: These short hairs are fine. Do not work them too much, or you will not have any left.

The Gold Ribbed Hare's Ear cont.

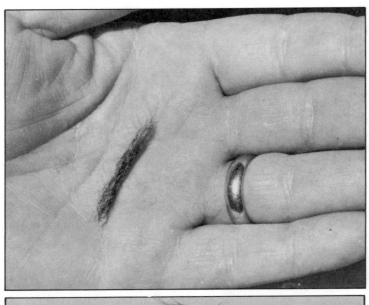

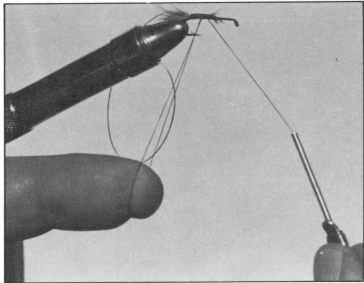

7. When the mat is formed, wet your palm *slightly* and gently roll the mat between your fingers and your palm to form a very loose "noodle." Set the noodle aside.

8. Form a loop of tying thread by grabbing the thread four or five inches below the hook and hold it with your left hand, while wrapping the bobbin thread over the hook end of the loop to the last wrap on your tail.

Note: *Poly Rosebrough developed this dubbing technique to tie his fuzzy nymphs effectively.*

The Gold Ribbed Hare's Ear cont.

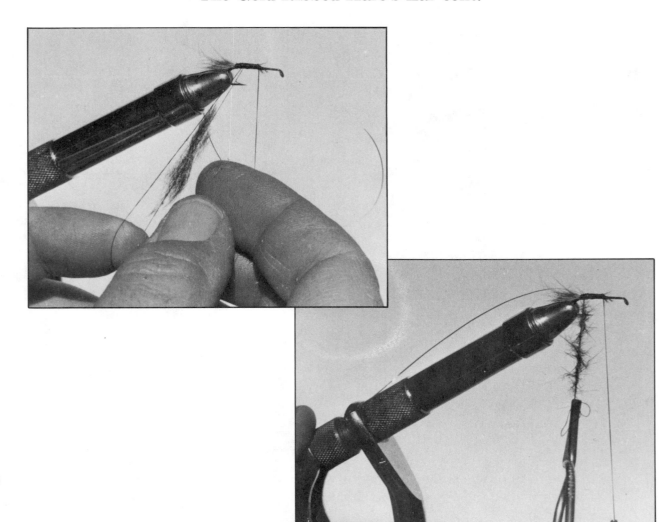

9. Advance thread half way to the eye on the hook shank.

10. Keeping the loop separated, apply dubbing wax to both sides of the loop.

11. Gently place noodle of hair between the strands of the loop. Bring strands of the loop together, trapping your noodle between the strands. Place the hackle pliers at the bottom of the strand where the noodle ends, trapping both strands of thread.

12. Begin to twist the loop by twisting the hackle pliers. The more you twist the loop, the tighter the strand of hair yarn will be formed.

13. When the hair yarn is tightly formed, wrap thread yarn to your thread at the mid point of the hook shank, and tie off. Cut off excess.

14. Rib the abdomen with the fine gold tinsel, spacing the wraps to give a segmented effect. Tie off and clip tinsel at the front end of abdomen.

The Gold Ribbed Hare's Ear cont.

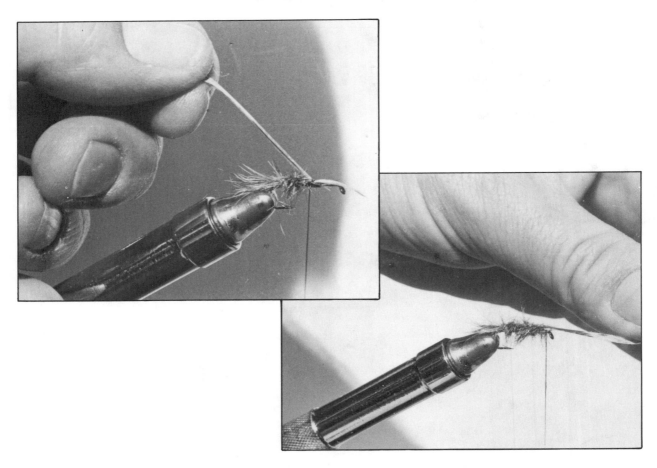

15. From a mottled brown turkey feather, usually a secondary wing feather, cut a section of barbules at the quill. This section should be approximately one-eight to one-quarter inch in width.

16. Tie in the tips of this section with the dull side up and the butts laying back over the abdomen. Wrap tips in with several thread wraps and clip excess tips. Make sure that the covert or wing case is positioned at the top of the hook.

17. Dub thorax using the same loop technique as the abdomen. Make noodle larger so that the thorax will be thicker.

18. Tie off thorax dubbing behind the eye leaving room for a head.

19. Cover the thorax with turkey covert, extending the feather over the eye. Tie in securely with four to five wraps. Clip remaining butts and finish head.

20. Half hitch and whip finish.

Note: *If you want a "fuzzy" nymph, gently pick out the hairs from your dubbed abdomen and thorax with a dubbing needle or your scissor points.*

WET FLIES & NYMPHS

Tying Tip #7

DUBBING IS SUPERIOR TO YARN OR OTHER PREPARED MATERIALS

The guard hairs and fuzzy appearance of a dubbed body give the impression of size without adding bulk. The individual hairs will gather air bubbles and give your fly a special translucent appearance in the water.

Additional Patterns

1. **Gold Ribbed Hares Ear — Wet**
   Hook: 3906B
   Thread: Black
   Tail: Brown Barbules
   Rib: Fine Gold Mylar Tinsel
   Body: Dubbed Hare's Ear Fur
   Wing: Slate Grey Wing Quill
   Segments tied wet fly style
   Hackle: Brown Barbules tied beard style

2. **Tellico Nymph**
   Hook: 3906B or 9671
   Thread: Black
   Tail: Brown Barbules
   Wing Case: Ringneck Pheasant Tail or Turkey Wing
   Rib: Peacock Herl
   Body: Yellow Floss
   Hackle: Brown

3. **Zug Bug Nymph**
   Hook: 3906B or 9671
   Thread: Black
   Tail: Peacock Sword Fibres
   Rib: Fine Gold Mylar Tinsel
   Body: Peacock Herl
   Hackle: Brown barbules tied beard style
   Wing Case: Lemon Wood Duck or Mallard Side tied in at head only.

4. **Silver Hilton**
   Hook: 3906B or 9671
   Thread: Black
   Tail: Grizzly Barbules
   Rib: Silver Mylar Tinsel
   Body: Black Chenille
   Wing: 2 Grizzly Hackle Tips curving away from shank
   Hackle: Grizzly tied wet style

DRY FLIES & STREAMERS

The Dry Fly is the purist's fly. There are many Fly Fishermen who won't use any fly other than one which floats. Ironically, most scientific studies show that trout obtain only 10-15% of their total diet on surface insects. Why then does the dry fly have the appeal to fishermen? I believe it has the appeal of providing the extra dimension of visual involvement. When you talk with a Fly Fishermen about dry fly fishing he will always talk of the thrill of "seeing" the fly as it's taken. Another appeal, which can be counted as visual also, is seeing a specific fish feeding and then presenting your fly to that particular fish.

There is also that part of Fly Fishing language referred to as "Matching the hatch." We've already discussed a hatch and the two other forms of the insect involved in the hatch, but the lore of fly fishing would lead you to believe that the only form of the insect is the adult. I suppose since it is in the air or on top of the water, we can more easily identify it and know what the trout are feeding on.

While nymph fishing is the most difficult technique to master and wet fly fishing can also be difficult, dry fly fishing demands casting accurracy and a "perfect" presentation. Tackle also becomes extremely important to the dry fly fisherman. A nymph fisherman may get away with short level leaders and relatively large flies. The dry fly fisherman will usually fish smaller flies and be forced to use tapered leaders and relatively fine tippets.

Streamers are those flies tied to imitate smaller fish making up a part of a trout's diet. Some are bait fish imitations while others are imitations of smaller game fish. Streamers are fished more like a lure than a fly, retrieving tight line against or cross current. This tight line retrieve usually means harder strikes. It can really be exciting to feel like your rod is being jerked out of your hand on a hard strike.

Streamers are also fun to tie. Most patterns use several colors and textures of materials to get the desired effect. Streamers are larger flies which are a relief to tie, especially to break the tedious tying of size 16 or 18 dry flies.

The real fun of Dry Flies or Streamers come from the "art" in the fly. When you finish a fly and it's tied properly, you can set back and admire your handywork. I am sure that you will be tempted to show off a few of your better patterns and enjoy accolades as the "artist."

DRY FLIES & STREAMERS

The Brown Bivisible

The Bivisible is the one fly I would choose as an all purpose dry fly. This dry fly may be tied in virtually any color and is effective in small, medium, and large sizes.

The Bivisible name is derived from the two highly visible portions of the fly. Since it is fluffy and high riding on the water, it is visible to the fish, and with the front portion being white or cream color, it is very visible to the fisherman.

The Brown Bivisible is tied with the following materials:

Hook: Mustad 94840
Head: Black thread
Tail: Brown barbules
Body: Brown neck hackle wrapped dry fly style from the tail forward. The final hackle, just behind the eye, is always white or cream.

To tie the Brown Bivisable, follow the steps listed below:

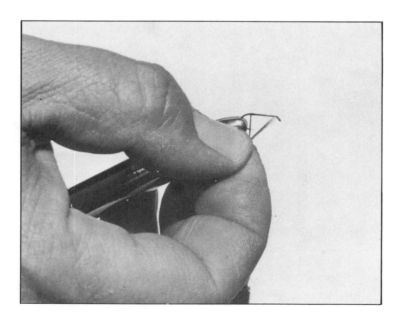

1. Select a brown hackle for your tail. Go to the sides of your neck or toward the top of the neck where you will find good quality feathers (no web) that are too long to use for most hackles.

2. Prepare a bundle of barbules for the tail. Make the tail as thick as practical and be certain that the tips of the barbules are even.

DRY FLIES & STREAMERS

The Brown Bivisible cont.

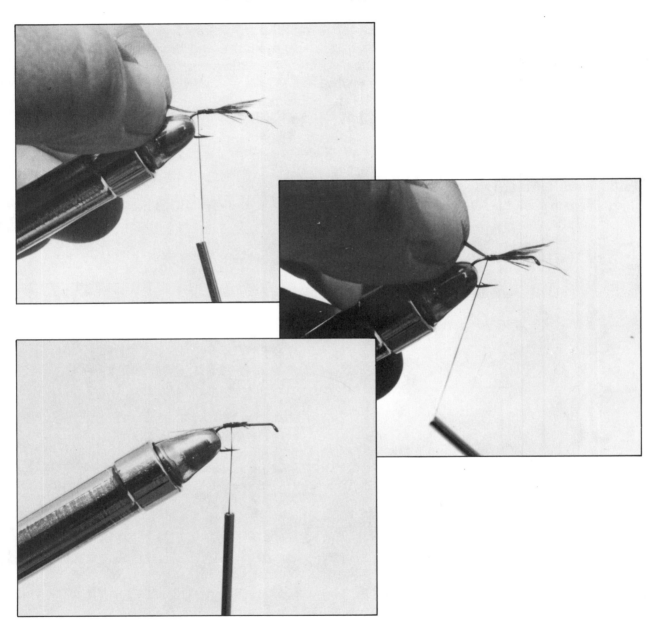

3. Size your tail and tie on. Make your first wrap at the starting position, the second and third wrap just slightly toward the eye, then wrap back toward the bend. As you wrap back, hold the bundle of tail up off the hook shank, lowering the tail gradually with each wrap until the final two wraps at the end of the shank. Hold the tail parallel with the hook shank. Make your last several wraps soft, with only a minimum of positive pressure holding the tail in line with the shank. Take two or three more wraps toward the eye until your thread is back at the starting position. Now let go of the tail with your left hand.

DRY FLIES & STREAMERS

The Brown Bivisible cont.

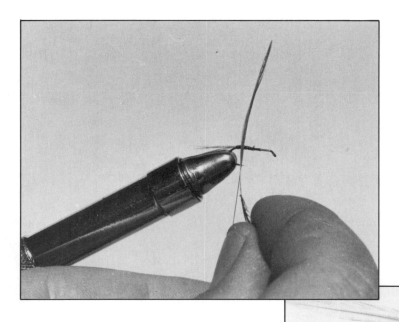

4. Select four neck hackles of the same barbule length and proper size for the hook you have chosen. Prepare all four feathers as hackles.

5. Tie in the first hackle feather dry fly style at the starting point and wrap your thread toward the bend to the tail, then back toward the eye past the hook point. The thread is advanced, not to the next tie off point as usual, but to get the bobbin and thread out of your way as you wrap the hackle.

6. Wrap the hackle dry fly style, with the concave side of the feather toward the eye, beginning your first wrap at the point the tail starts, covering the last wrap of thread on the tail. Be careful—do not ruin your tail. Continue to wrap forward toward the eye, making each wrap directly in front of the last one.

The Brown Bivisible cont.

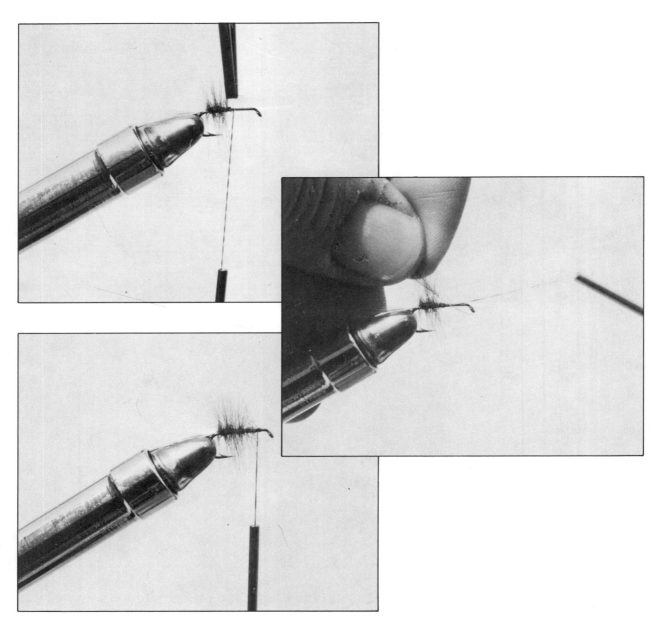

7. When you reach the tip of your hackle and can wrap no more, **unwrap** your thread back to the hackle and tie off. Clip excess hackle and take two more wraps to cover the stubs.

8. Tie in your second hackle directly in front of the finished first hackle and advance thread to get it out of your way. Wrap your second hackle just as you did your first. Tie off and clip excess feather.

9. Tie in the third and fourth hackle, if necessary, and wrap forward to behind the eye. Leave room enough for one more hackle and a head.

The Brown Bivisible cont.

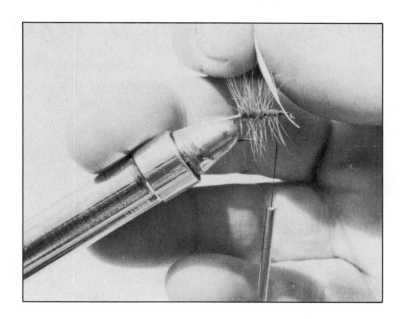

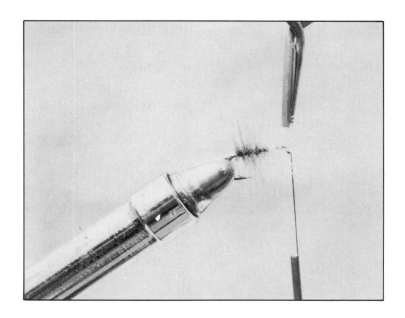

10. Select proper white or cream hackle. Prepare and tie in dry fly style in front of last brown hackle.

11. Wrap white feather dry fly style and tie off. Clip excess tip and finish head.

12. Half hitch and whip finish.

DRY FLIES & STREAMERS

Tying Tip #8

SELECTION OF MATERIAL IS THE KEY TO A GOOD FLY

Take your time when selecting materials. Those materials are the key to a fly which will look better and fish effectively. Not only will the materials determine the visual effect, but they will also determine whether the fly will float properly or sink.

Additional Patterns

1 . **Orange Asher**
   Hook: 94840
   Thread: Black
   Tail: None
   Body: Orange Floss
   Hackle: Brown Feather palmered over floss body

2. **Black Bivisible**
   Hook: 94840
   Thread: Black
   Tail: Black Barbules
   Body: None
   Hackle: Black Hackle wound dry fly style along shank—final feather white or cream at front

3. **Badger Bivisible**
   Hook: 94840
   Thread: Black
   Tail: Badger Barbules
   Body: None
   Hackle: Badger Hackle (cream with dark center) wound dry fly style along shank—final feather white or cream at front

4. **Dun Bivisible***
   Hook: 94840
   Thread: Black
   Tail: Dun Barbules
   Body: None
   Hackle: Blue Dun Hackle wound dry fly style along shank—final feather white or cream at front.

*Dun is Fly Tying color for blue-grey.

DRY FLIES & STREAMERS

The Grizzly Mosquito

This is my oldest son, Mike's, favorite fly. He used this successfully in southern Colorado where he has spent the summers leading backpacking trips. Used in small streams and beaver dams, this dry fly, while even fished wet part of the time, produced trout regularly.

The Grizzly Mosquito is tied with the following materials:

Hook: Mustad 94840
Head: Black
Tail: Grizzly barbules
Body: Grizzly hackle quill
Hackle: Grizzly neck

To tie the Grizzly Mosquito, follow the steps listed below.

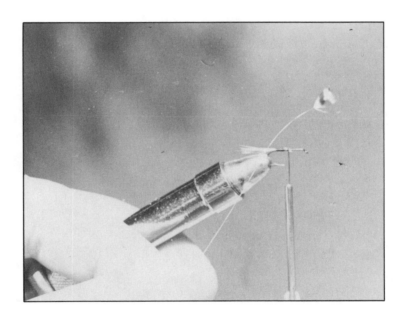

1. Select and prepare grizzly barbule tail, size, and tie in.
2. Select a long neck hackle from the top of a grizzly neck or saddle, and strip all of the barbules from the quill.
3. Tie in the quill tip and advance the thread to behind the eye.

DRY FLIES & STREAMERS

The Grizzly Mosquito cont.

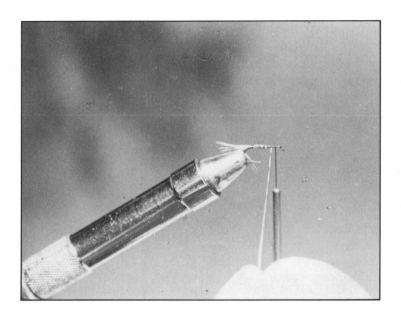

4. Carefully wrap the hackle quill toward the eye. Do not put any excess pressure on the quill as it is fragile. Make close wraps, butting each wrap into the previous one. Note that the first wraps seem to not advance much, but as you continue to wrap, the quill diameter increases, and you get a nice even, tapered body.

5. Tie off the excess quill butt behind the eye. Leave room for the hackle and the head. Because the quill butt is stiff, it needs several wraps to ensure that it will not come loose. Be sure you cover all the stub when you tie and clip.

6. Select two properly sized hackle feathers and tie in dry fly style.

DRY FLIES & STREAMERS

The Grizzly Mosquito cont.

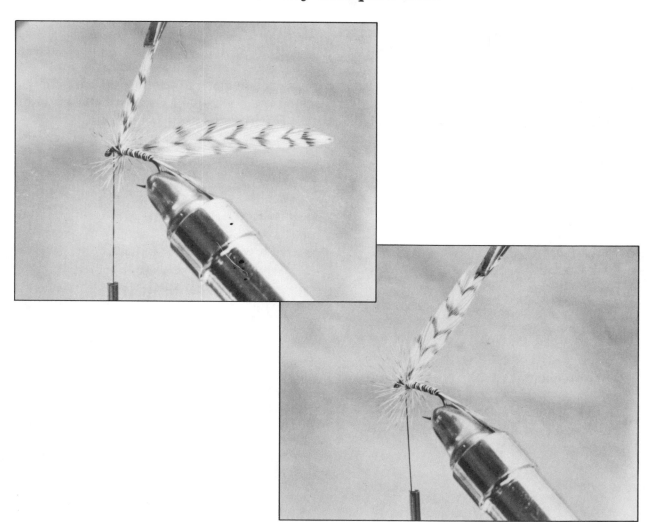

7. Wrap the first hackle, making the first wrap directly in front of your finished quill body. Wrap hackle as close as possible dry fly style.

8. Tie off first hackle. Make sure you still have a head and room to tie off the second hackle.

9. Wrap the second hackle. Make your first wrap behind the first hackle and in front of the quill body, gathering the hackle barbules sticking out toward the tail, if any, and continue to wrap in a forward motion through the first hackle.

10. As you wrap through the first hackle, you must weave the feather back and forth slightly to keep from crushing the first hackle. Finish this hackle wrap in front of the existing hackle and tie off carefully.

11. Cut excess hackle tip and finish the head, keeping the head as small as possible.

12. Half hitch and whip finish.

DRY FLIES & STREAMERS

Tying Tip #9

DRY FLY HACKLE SHOULD BE DENSE

Assuming proper selection of materials, the difference between a good dry fly and one that does not float or floats for only a short time is the density of the hackle. To achieve density, try to wrap the hackle in as small a space on the hook shank as possible. This density gives support to each barbule and balances the fly properly while maintaining fly symmetry.

Additional Patterns

1. **Cream Varient**
   Hook: 94840
   Thread: Black
   Tail: Cream Barbules
   Body: Cream Hackle Stem
   Hackle: Cream—slightly oversized

2. **Brown Varient**
   Hook: 94840
   Thread: Black
   Tail: Brown Barbules
   Body: Brown Hackle Stem
   Hackle: Brown Neck—slightly
        oversized

3. **Ginger Quill**
   Hook: 94840
   Thread: Black or Cream
   Wing: Grey Quill Segments—upright
        and divided
   Tail: Cream (or Light Ginger) Barbules
   Body: Stripped Peacock Quill
        (or Cream Hackle Quill)
   Hackle: Cream or Lt. Ginger

4. **Quill Gordon**
   Hook: 94840
   Thread: Black
   Tail: Dun Hackle Fibres
   Body: Stripped Peacock Quill*
   Wing: Upright Split Mallard Side
        Feather dyed woodduck color
   Hackle: Med. Blue Dun

*Use pencil eraser to remove fuzz from entire length of peacock herl.

DRY FLIES & STREAMERS

The Adams

The Adams is probably the most popular dry fly in the West. It was originally tied as a Caddis imitation, but I find that it fits almost any conditions and is used successfully even in some May Fly hatches.

The Adams is tied with the following materials:

Hook: Mustad 94840
Head: Black
Tail: Mixed brown and grizzly barbules
Body: Lightly dubbed grey synthetic yard (or Muskrat fur)
Wings: Grizzly hackle tips
Hackle: Mixed brown and grizzly neck

To tie the Adams, follow the steps listed below.

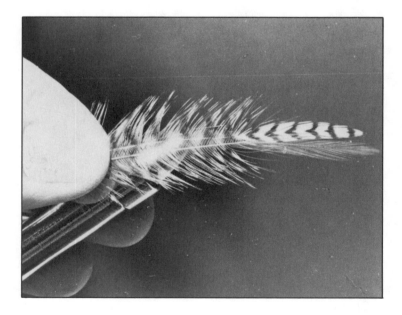

1. Select one grizzly and one brown feather suitable for tailing. Prepare the tail as you normally would. However, this time pull the barbules from two feathers, one brown and one grizzly, at the same time. Be sure that the barbule tips are lined up and even before you pull them off.

2. Size the tail and tie in. Cut off the excess and advance your thread to a point half way to the eye plus two or three wraps.

DRY FLIES & STREAMERS

The Adams cont.

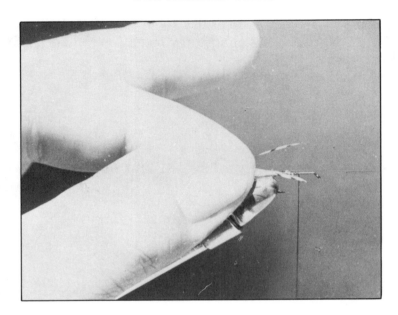

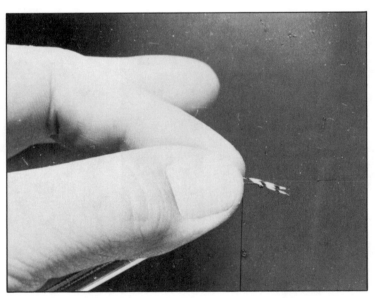

3. Select two grizzly hackles for wings. These should be the same size. They should be feathers from the side or bottom of the neck, and ones not usually used for hackle.

4. Size the wings by holding the hackle tips along the top of the hook shank. The wings should be slightly longer than the shank since we are using a standard length hook shank. Strip the lower barbules and fuzz below the tip lengths selected.

5. Hold both hackle tips in your left thumb and forefinger with the convex sides together. Place the tips on edge with the bottom of the wings just above your thread position and the tip forward over the eye.

The Adams cont.

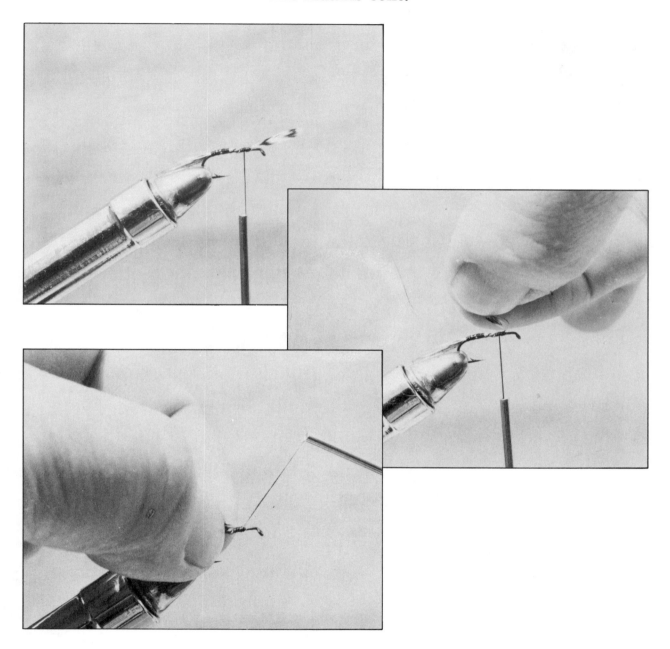

6. Tie in the wings carefully so they do not roll away from you. Take two or three wraps slightly forward toward the eye. Clip the excess butts.

7. Move you left thumb and forefinger over the eye to the tips, and grasping the tips, pull the wings up and straight back toward the bend of the hook. Lay the wings slightly back over the shank, and tie a wedge with your thread directly in front of the wings. Tie the wedge with six or eight wraps.

8. Let go of the wings, and they should stand straight up and spread apart.

The Adams cont.

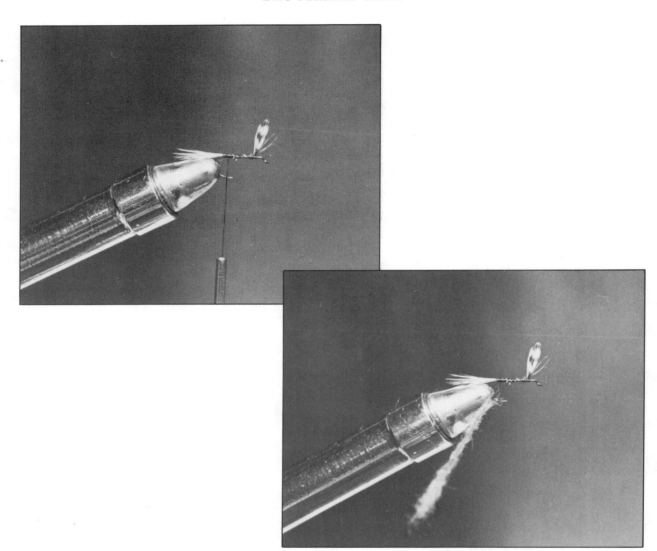

9. Do not worry if they are not exactly straight. We will cure this in the next several steps.

10. Gently X or figure eight the wings by wrapping the thread between the wings. Your first wrap is from the front to the back of the wings, holding the off side, or far side, wing in position. Take two wraps; now hold the wing closest to you and take your thread between the wings from back to front two times.

11. Wrap thread back to normal starting position.

12. Prepare a thin mat of grey dubbing material—narrower at the top and wider at the bottom. Remember, you want a thin body so use very little material. Dub the body so that you have a nice, even tapered body. Cut off excess material leaving room behind the wings to tie in the hackles.

DRY FLIES & STREAMERS

The Adams cont.

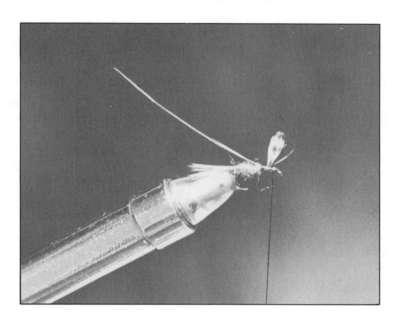

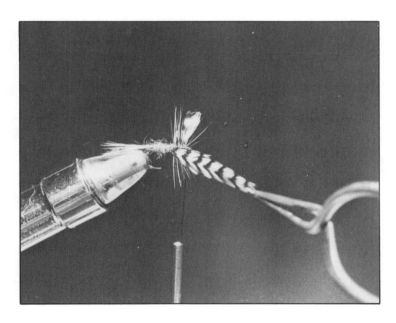

13. Select, prepare, and tie in one brown hackle and one grizzly hackle feather of the same appropriate barbule length.
14. Wrap each feather dry fly style beginning behind the wing and finishing just behind the eye. Tie each off.
15. Half hitch and whip finish.

DRY FLIES & STREAMERS

Tying Tip #10

DRY FLY WINGS SHOULD BE SLIGHTLY LONGER
THAN THE HACKLE

The tiny extra bit of length in dry fly wings will make the wings distinct. This extra length will also aid in keeping wings separated while wrapping hackles.

Additional Patterns

1. **FFF May Fly**
   Hook: 94840
   Thread: Black
   Tail: Black & Brown Barbules mixed
   Body: Dubbed Dark Brown Fur
   Rib: Light Color Thread (tan or cream)
   Wing: Grizzly Hackle Tips
   Hackle: Brown and Black mixed

2. **Grey Fox Varient**
   Hook: 94840
   Thread: Black
   Tail: Lt. Brown or Ginger Barbules
   Body: Cream Hackle Stem
   Wing: None
   Hackle: Ginger, Lt. Brown & Grizzly mixed

3. **Joe's Hopper**
   Hook: 94840
   Thread: Black
   Tail: Red Hackle Fibres
   Body: Yellow Chenille, with small loop at back. Brown Saddle Hackle palmered over body and trimmed.
   Wing: Mottled Turkey over length of body (Trim to shape)
   Hackle: Brown and Grizzly mixed

4. **Blue Winged Olive**
   Hook: 94840
   Thread: Black or Olive
   Tail: Blue Dun
   Body: Yellowish Olive dubbed Fur or Poly
   Wing: Blue Dun Hackle Tips
   Hackle: Medium Blue Dun

DRY FLIES & STREAMERS

The Elk Hair Caddis

The Elk Hair Caddis, or the Elk Wing Caddis, is a newcomer to the fly fishing scene. It has become very popular since it was introduced a short time ago.

The West has more Caddis flies; therefore this and other similar patterns have been quickly adopted by western fly fishermen.

The Elk Hair Caddis is tied with the following materials:

Hook: Mustad 94840
Body: Light yellow dubbing
Hackle: Brown hackle, palmered over body
Wing: Elk hair
Head: Clipped butts of elk hair

To tie the Elk Hair Caddis, follow the steps listed below:

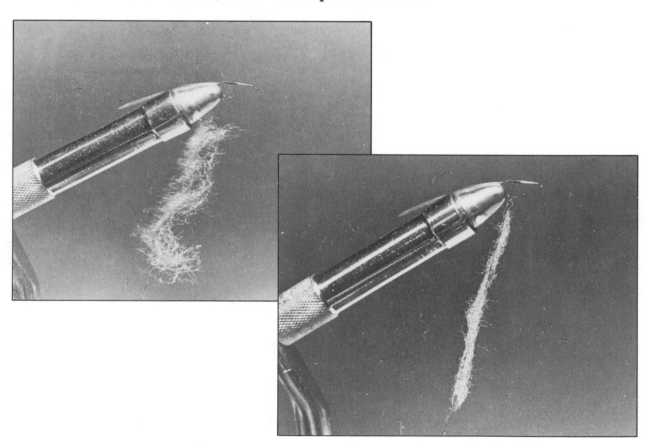

1. Select, prepare, and tie in a proper sized hackle feather at the bend of the hook.
2. Dub light yellow synthetic yarn, which has been clipped into short pieces and separated into fuzzy dubbing to behind the eye. Leave a lot of room for the wing and head.

The Elk Hair Caddis cont.

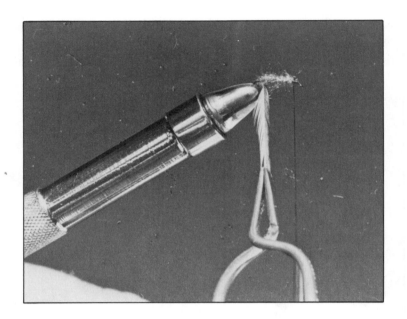

3. Palmer the brown hackle, and tie off at the front end of the body.
4. Clip a bundle of elk hair about the size of a match stick. Remove the fuzz and short hair by holding the tips firmly in one hand while fluffing the butts with your forefinger.
5. Place elk hair in hair stacker and even the tips.
6. Gently remove the cap from the hair stacker while holding the stacker horizontally, and grasp the tips between your left thumb and forefinger.

DRY FLIES & STREAMERS

The Elk Hair Caddis cont.

7. Grab the butts between your right thumb and forefinger and size the wing. The wing should be longer than normal, extending past the bend of the hook.

8. Grab the sized wing between your left thumb and forefinger, and place it in position on top of the hook to tie in.

9. Your thread should be half way between the eye and the end of the body.

10. Hold the wing firmly in your left hand and wrap thread. Your first wrap should be firm but not tight. Make two or three wraps toward the eye, increasing the pressure with each wrap. Now wrap back toward the bend with decreasing pressure until your last wrap back at the front end of the body is only tight enough to hold the bundle of hair together but not tight enough to flare the hair.

The Elk Hair Caddis cont.

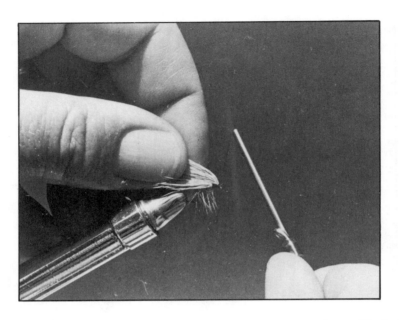

11. Wrap back toward the eye with increasing pressure to a point still short of the eye. Lift the elk hair butts up and wrap underneath the butts while holding the butts straight up and off the hook shank.

12. Clip the elk butts leaving a stub of butts sticking up over the eye. The stub should be reasonably prominent—an eighth of an inch long.

13. Half hitch and whip finish.

DRY FLIES & STREAMERS

Tying Tip #11

SYNTHETIC MATERIALS HAVE THEIR PLACE

Not only do synthetics offer a wide color choice, but they are economical and easy to use and have a specific gravity less than water. This means added float for your dry fly. When tail and hackle are not supporting your dry fly, as in the Elk Hair Caddis, synthetic materials will aid in keeping your fly afloat.

Additional Patterns

1. **Coachman Trude**
   Hook: 94840
   Thread: Black
   Tail: Golden Pheasant Tippets
   Body: Peacock Herl
   Wing: White Calf Tail—trude style (down over body)
   Hackle: Brown Redgame Hackle tied dry fly style (at least 2 feathers)

2. **Colorado King**
   Hook: 94840
   Thread: Black
   Tail: 2 Peccary Fibres Spread (or 2 stiff moose body hairs)
   Body: Dubbed Muskrat
   Rib: Grizzly Hackle—palmered
   Wing: Deer Body Hair tied like Elk Hair Caddis

3. **Kings River Caddis**
   Hook: 94840
   Thread: Black
   Tail: None
   Body: Orange Yarn or Floss
   Rib: Brown Hackle tied palmer style and clipped short
   Wing: Rolled Mottled Turkey Wing
   Hackle: Brown Neck Hackle

4. **Blonde Trude**
   Hook: 94840
   Thread: Black or White
   Tail: Cream Hackle Barbules
   Body: Dubbed Cream Fur
   Wing: Light Elk Body Hair tied trude style (one clump tied down over body)
   Hackle: Cream Neck Hackle

DRY FLIES & STREAMERS

The Royal Wulff

No collection of dry flies is complete without a sample of the Royal Coachman. Every time you tie one of the many Coachman patterns, you are sharing a fly fishing heritage that spans centuries.

The true Royal Coachman pattern is still very effective; however, the pattern is not very durable and is difficult to keep afloat in heavy water. Lee Wulff influenced fly tying by developing the Wulff style pattern which is a higher riding, more durable dry fly.

The Royal Wulff is tied with the following materials:

Hook: Mustad 94840
Head: Black
Tail: Deer body hair
Egg Sack: Peacock herl
Body: Red floss
Thorax: Peacock herl
Hackle: Brown neck
Wings: White calf tail

To tie the Royal Wulff, follow the steps listed below:

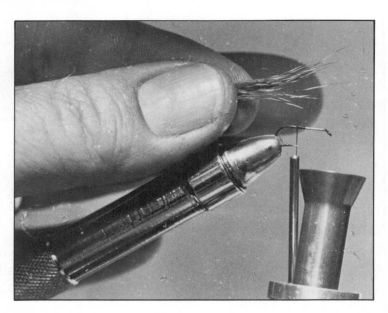

1. Clip a small bundle of deer hair and prepare it just as you did elk hair—getting rid of the fuzz and fur at the base of the hair and eliminating the short hairs.
2. Using your hair stacker, stack the tail material and select a small bundle of eight to twelve hairs.
3. Size your tail and hold the bundle firmly between your left thumb and forefinger on top of the hook.

DRY FLIES & STREAMERS

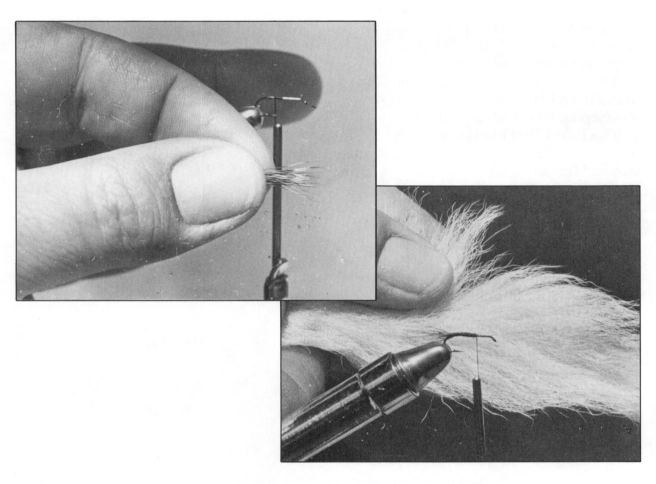

4. Make your first wrap at the starting point with positive pressure.

5. With increasing pressure, wrap slightly toward the eye. Four or five wraps are sufficient. Your last wrap should be very firm. The hair butts will flare, but do not worry. You will trim these excess butts.

6. Wrap firmly back to your starting position.

7. With decreasing pressure, wrap the thread toward the bend of the hook, making sure that the tail is on top of the hook as you lift the ends and gradually lower the ends.

8. The last wrap at the end of your tail should be loose. Too much pressure will flare the hair and make your tail spread. Wrap the thread back to the starting position.

9. Clip the excess butts carefully, and wrap the thread over the butts to the bare hook shank and then back to the starting position. Firmly advance the thread to a point midway toward the eye plus two or three wraps.

10. Clip a bundle of hair from the white calf tail about one-half the diameter of a lead pencil. The best hairs for wings will be along the sides of the calf tail, not at the tip where the hairs start to curl.

The Royal Wulff cont.

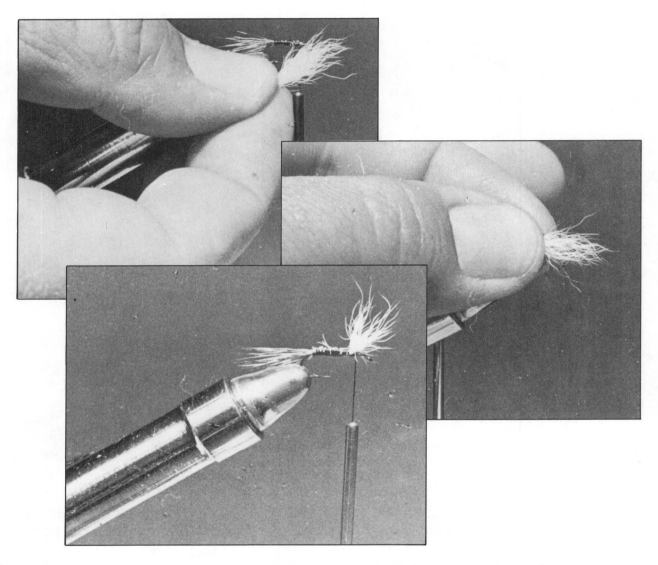

11. Holding the tips in your left hand, firmly fluff the butts and get rid of the short hairs.

12. Pluck the long and curly hairs from the tips. The tips should not be exactly even. This uneven spread adds to the effect of calf tail wings and is desirable.

13. Size the wings. Holding the butts in your left fingers, tie in wings at the point just beyond the halfway point.

14. Wrap firmly for four or five wraps, advancing the thread slightly toward the eye. With your left fingers, reach forward over the eye and grab the tips and pull them straight back and angled toward the tail. Wrap a wedge in front of the wings with eight or ten wraps. Let go of the tips, and your wings should stand up straight off the shank. Take the thread to behind the wings. Cut the excess butts of wing, angling your scissors so that you make a tapered cut rather than a square cut at right angles to the shank.

The Royal Wulff cont.

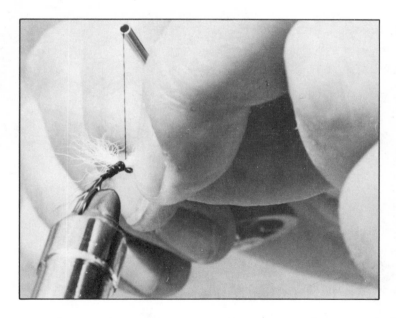

15. With your left thumb and forefinger, separate the wing bundle into two approximately even wings. Firmly holding the far side wing, carefully wrap from the back of the wing to the front several times finishing in front. Now grab the near wing and wrap between the wings from front to back several times. This procedure is called xing the wings.

16. Wrap back of the wing over your butts. Tapering your wraps so that when you finish, the body behind the wings is gradually sloped back toward the tail. Finish with your thread just behind the wings.

The Royal Wulff cont.

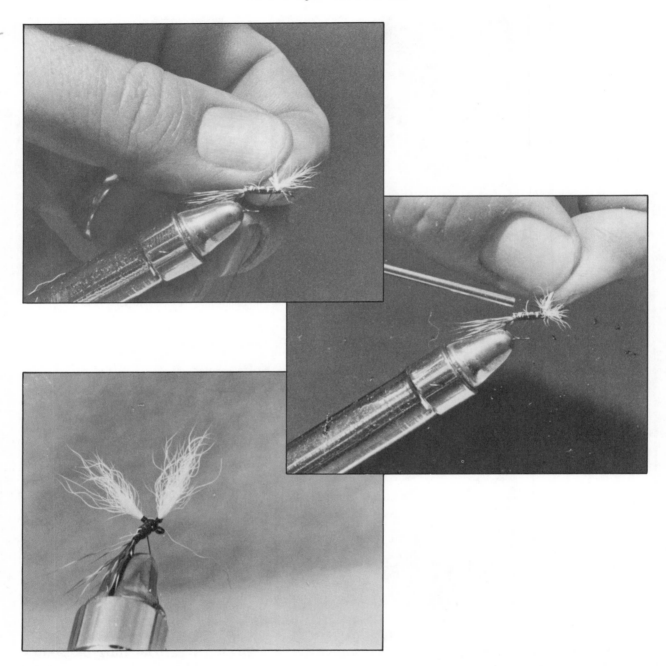

17. Grab the far side wing firmly, and while holding the wing in position, tie the thread around the butts, parallelling the hook shank for three or four wraps. Finish the parallel wrap in front, and wrap two or three firm wraps in front of the wings while still holding the wing in the desired position. Repeat the parallel wrap on the near wing, finishing in back. Wrap firmly two or three times in back of the wings. Take your thread back to the starting position.

The Royal Wulff cont.

18. Tie in one stand of peacock, and wrap back to the tail. Be sure that you do not ruin the tail. Wrap herl to cover thread wraps at tail and make a very narrow, fluffy eggsack. Tie off herl and clip the excess butt.

19. Tie in one strand of red floss and advance your thread to behind the wings. Wrap the floss evenly to just short of your wing and tie off. Clip the excess.

20. Tie in the herl again at the front of the red body, wrapping slightly back into the body. Wrap herl, forming a narrow, fluffy thorax. Tie off and cut excess. You should still have a little room behind the wings to tie in the hackle.

The Royal Wulff cont.

21. Select and prepare two to four brown hackle feathers of proper length, and tie in dry fly style.

22. Wrap hackle feather dry fly style, concentrating on making as narrow and fluffy a hackle as possible.

23. Clip off excess after each hackle is wrapped. After all hackles have been wrapped and tied off, finish head, half hitch, and whip finish.

DRY FLIES & STREAMERS

Tying Tip #12

FIRMLY FIX ALL MATERIALS TO THE HOOK SHANK

When using bulky materials to tie a fly, it is important to tie on the materials, clip the excess, and then take the thread to the bare hook shank for several wraps and then back up on to the materials. This will keep your materials from rolling around the hook.

Additional Patterns

1. **Grizzly Wulff**
   Hook: 94840
   Thread: Black
   Tail: Deer Hair or Buck Tail
   Body: Yellow Floss
   Wing: Deer Hair
   Hackle: Mixed Brown & Grizzly

2. **Black Wulff**
   Hook: 94840
   Thread: Black
   Tail: Black Deer Hair or Moose Body
   Body: Red Floss
   Wing: Dark Deer
   Hackle: Black Neck

3. **H & L Varient**
   Hook: 94840
   Thread: Black
   Tail: White Calf Tail
   Body: Back ½ Stripped Peacock Quill
   Front ½ Peacock Herl
   Wing: White Calf Tail—upright and split
   Hackle: Brown Neck

4. **White Wulff**
   Hook: 94840
   Thread: Black or White
   Tail: White Calf Tail
   Body: White Dubbed Fur or Poly
   Wing: White Calf Tail
   Hackle: Cream or Badger (at least 2 feathers tied dry fly style)

DRY FLIES & STREAMERS

The Muddler Minnow

The Muddler Minnow was originally tied to imitate the Sculpin, a small, ugly fish preyed upon by a number of larger fish including the trout. The Muddler Minnow has become a widely accepted streamer. While it successfully imitates a minnow, the Muddler patterns may often be taken for a grasshopper or large stonefly. The buoyancy of deer hair adds fishing characteristics to this streamer that truly makes it unique.

The Muddler Minnow is tied using the following materials:

Hook: Mustad 38941
Thread: Black
Tail: Mottled turkey
Body: Gold mylar tinsel
Underwing: White calf tail or squirrel tail
Wing: Mottled turkey
Head: Spun deer hair clipped in front with strands extending to bend

To tie the Muddler Minnow, follow the steps listed below.

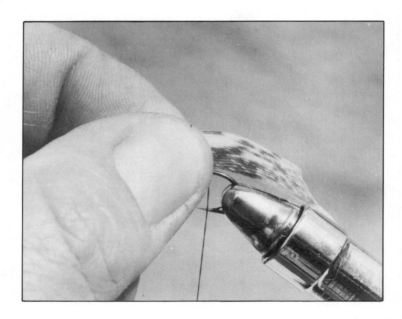

1. Select a section of turkey quill approximately the heighth of the hook gap.
2. Take the thread back to the end of the shank. (Not starting position)
3. Size the tail, about one to one and one-half times the hook gap, and hold firmly between your left thumb and forefinger. Set the feather with the curve down on its edge on top of the shank.

The Muddler Minnow cont.

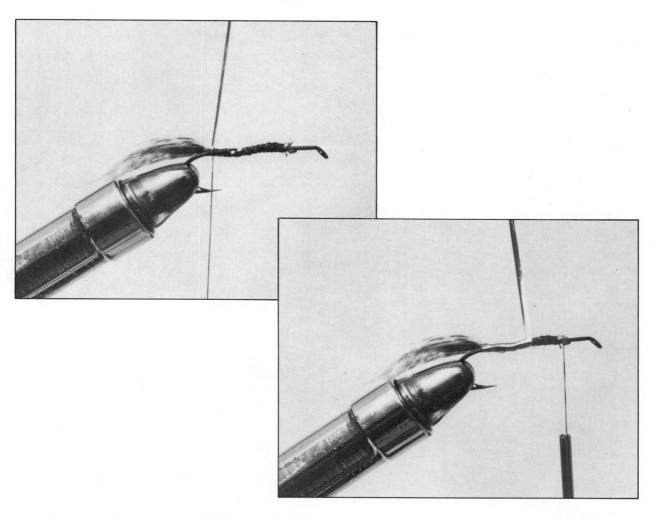

4. Take two loose wraps slowly, trapping the thread between your thumb on one side and your forefinger on the other side. Trap these wraps between your finger or thumb and the tail feather.
5. Pull straight down with the bobbin, increasing the pressure until the two wraps are cinched tight. Do not let go of the tail.
6. Make four or five wraps toward the eye. Let go of the tail. It should be straight off the hook shank and not rolled. The tip of the feather will be curved, but that is inherent in the feather.
7. Tie in wide mylar tinsel, silver side up, and wrap your thread to a point about two-thirds of the way toward the eye. Wrap over the tail butts and clip excess, if any. Wrap the tinsel to your thread, tie in, and clip excess.

Note: *If the feather rolls, you probably did not hold the feather tight enough as you took your first two wraps and pulled straight down.*

The Muddler Minnow cont.

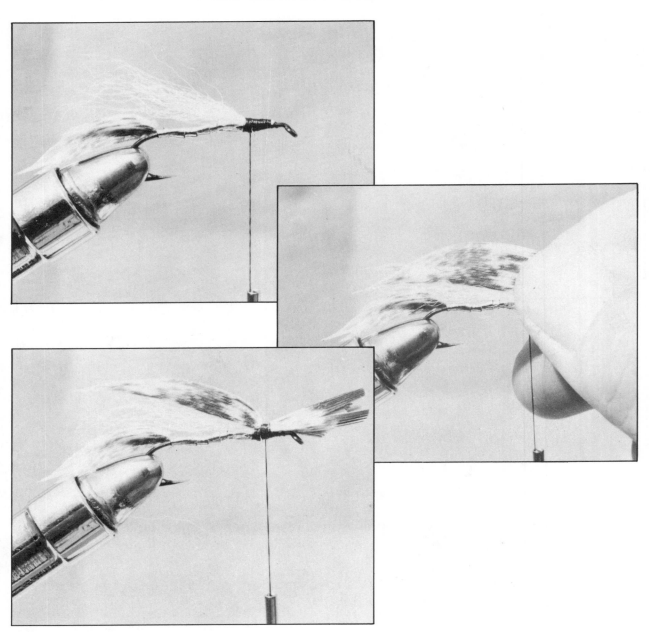

8. Tie in a small bunch of calf tail, with tips extending almost to the bend. Clip off excess carefully and cover the butts with thread. Caution: Do not build up thread or excess material in front of the underwings.

9. Bring thread to the last wrap on the underwing closest to the body.

10. Tie in a pair of turkey quill segments, taken from opposite sides of the same turkey quill. The longest tip should be next to the shank so that the wing curves down. Use the same technique you used to tie in the tail.

DRY FLIES & STREAMERS

The Muddler Minnow cont.

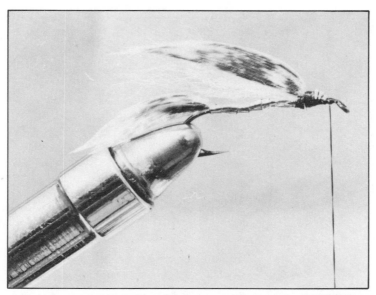

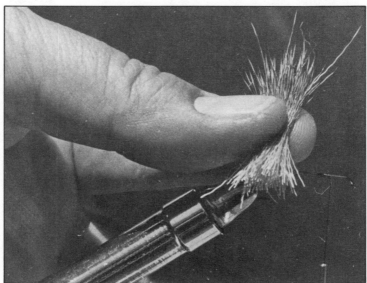

11. Clip the excess wing butts and cover them carefully with the thread. Make sure you take the thread to the bare hook shank and back to the butts. This will secure the wing to the hook shank and prevent wing rotation as you spin hair.

12. Half hitch your thread in a position half way between the wing and the eye. You should still have one-quarter to three-eights inch left behind the eye.

13. Cut a bundle of deer hair slightly smaller than a pencil diameter. Fluff the ends and get rid of the fuzz.

14. Place the bundle of deer hair on top of the hook shank with the tips toward the bend and extending just past the bend.

The Muddler Minnow cont.

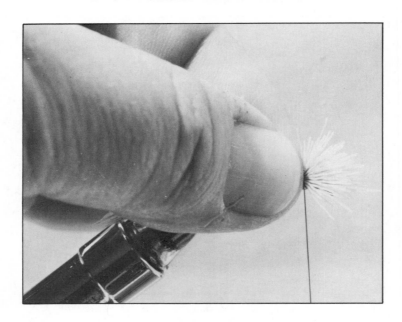

15. While holding the hook tightly between the left thumb and forefinger, take two loose wraps directly in front of your fingers.

16. Pull straight down with the bobbin, increasing the pressure until the hair begins to flare noticeably. Continue to pull straight down removing your left fingers. Hair should roll around the hook.

17. Take two or three more wraps, increasing the pressure as the hair continues to spiral around the hook shank. The hair should now be evenly spread around the hook.

The Muddler Minnow cont.

18. While maintaining tension on the thread, reach in front of the eye and pull all the butts back to free the eye. You may have to work the butts a little to free the eye.

19. Gently work your thread through the hair and tie immediately behind the eye several times. Pull the butts back toward the bend making a tighter bunch and continue to wrap back slightly.

20. Finish the head behind the eye. Half hitch and whip finish.

21. After cutting the thread, you can now clip the hair head to shape.

22. The head should be round—a bit flatter on top, straight across the front, and tapered from the front back to the wing.

23. Trim the sides, top, and bottom behind the head by clipping those strands that do not lie flat against the body.

DRY FLIES & STREAMERS

Tying Tip #13

TRIM HAIR SLOWLY, A LITTLE AT A TIME

You can always cut a little more, but once cut, it is impossible to add more at this point. The larger a muddler head is the more floating tendency you will get; the smaller the head, the more readily it will sink.

Additional Patterns

1. **The Letort Hopper**
   Hook: 9671, 38941 or 9672
   Thread: Black
   Body: Yellow Fur or Poly
   Wing: Mottled Turkey over entire body and deer hair spun with head clipped short and hair covering top of wing and down to mid body on sides

2. **White Maribou Muddler**
   Hook: 38941 or 9672
   Thread: Black
   Tail: Red Hackle Fibres
   Body: Silver Tinsel (or tinsel chenille)
   Wing: White Maribou topped with 2 to 4 strands of peacock herl
   Head: Spun Deer Body Hair clipped to shape, leaving strands extending toward bend

3. **Deer Hair Hopper**
   Hook: 38941 or 9672
   Thread: Black
   Tail: Red Hackle Fibres
   Body: Yellow Deer Body Hair, spun and clipped to shape
   Wing: Brown Mottled Turkey
   Hackle: Brown and Grizzly mixed

4. **Black Maribou Muddler**
   Hook: 38941 or 9672
   Thread: Black
   Tail: Red Hackle Fibres
   Body: Silver Tinsel
   Wing: Black Maribou topped with 2 to 4 peacock herl strands
   Head: Spun Deer Body Hair tied and clipped muddler style

DRY FLIES & STREAMERS

The Humpy

Caddis imitations have been the last to gain favor among fishermen, particularly the traditionalist. However, as most fly fishermen try the Humpy, they quickly include it among their favorite patterns.

The Humpy is normally tied with a yellow or red underbody. However, if it is tied with a no floss underbody, it is commonly known as the Goofus Bug. If tied with a red underbody and white calf tail wings, it is known as the Royal Humpy. We will tie the Elk Hair Humpy, substituting elk hair for deer hair in the original pattern. The techniques are similar for all patterns.

The Elk Hair Humpy is tied using the following materials:

Hook: Mustad 94840
Head: Black
Tail: Elk body hair
Underbody: Yellow floss or Red floss
Body: Elk hair drawn over the length of underbody as a hump or covert
Hackle: Brown neck
Wings: Elk hair tips

To tie the Humpy, follow the steps listed below.

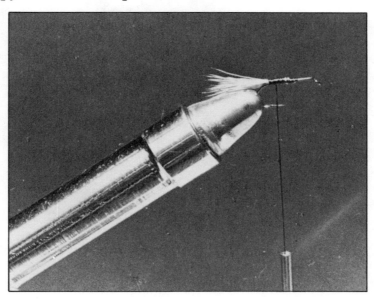

1. Select a small bundle of elk hair, stack to even the tips, and tie in just as you tied in the deer hair for the Royal Wulff. Cut off the butts about half way up the shank and wrap over with thread.

   The next step is the most critical when tying a Humpy, and it gives tyers more problems than any other step. The key to this step is the proper length of elk hair. The same bunch of hair will be used for the hump as well as the wings.

The Humpy cont.

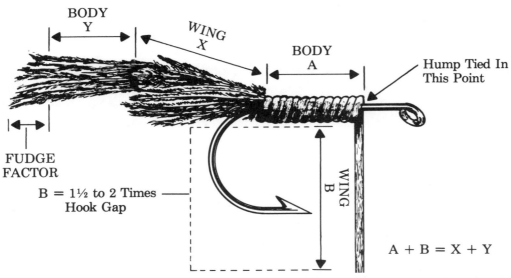

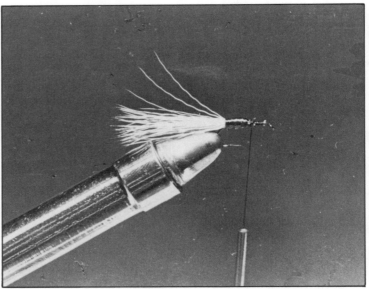

2. Cut a bundle of elk hair and carefully prepare it, making sure that all of the short ends are fluffed out. Hold the bundle close to the tips and vigorously fluff the butts until you have a bundle of hair approximately the same length.

3. Stack the hair to even the tips and size the bundle as shown above. The length of this bundle should be sufficient to cover the body with enough length left to stand upright and form the elk hair wings. The fudge factor is added to allow for space used when folding over and tying in.

4. Tie in the sized elk hair bundle, and wrap back to the tail. Do not wrap past the tail. Cut excess butts at an angle and wrap in, taking your thread to a bare shank and back again to the starting position.

DRY FLIES & STREAMERS

The Humpy cont.

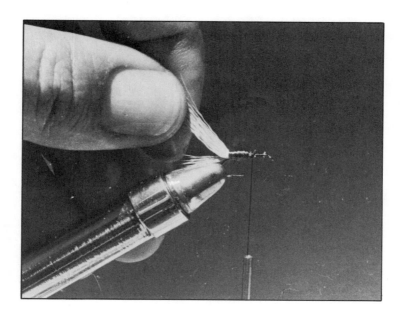

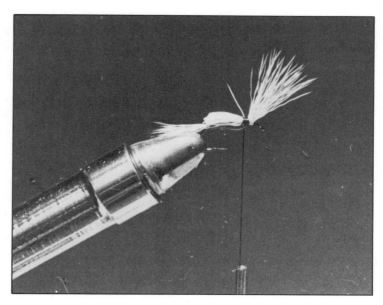

5. Tie in the yellow floss and wrap to the half way point. Tie off floss and cut excess. Be sure that floss covers all the thread wraps at the tail.

6. Pull wings up and over the body for the hump and tie in at the half way point. Make two or three more wraps toward the eye. Make sure that the tips stay on top of the shank.

Note: If you grab just the tips of the hump hair as you pull it over, you will leave the tail behind.

The Humpy cont.

7. Pull the wings back and tie a wedge of thread in front of the wings. Separate into bundles and X as you did with the calf tail wings. Do the parallel butt wraps on each wing as you did on calf tail wings, (Royal Wulff).

8. Select and prepare two or three brown hackle feathers of proper size, tie in, and wrap hackles dry fly style.

9. Finish head, half hitch, and whip finish.

DRY FLIES & STREAMERS

Tying Tip #14

THE AMOUNT OF MATERIAL CHOSEN WILL GREATLY AFFECT YOUR FINISHED PRODUCT

We have talked about quality and proportion of material, but quantity is also important. When you use too much of a material, the result is an imbalanced fly. If too little is used, the parts will not be distinct. Take care in selecting the proper amount of material.

Additional Patterns

1. **The Royal Humpy**
   Hook: 94840
   Thread: Black
   Tail: Dark Moose Body Hair
   Underbody: Red Floss
   Body: Dark Moose over Red Floss
   Wing: White Calf Tail
   Hackle: Brown Neck Hackle

2. **Humpy Trude**
   Hook: 94840
   Thread: Black
   Tail: Dark Deer Body Hair or Moose
   Underbody: Floss Yellow, Red, Brown or Green (your choice)
   Body: Deer or Elk Body Hair over Floss
   Wing: White Calf Tail (tied down—trude style)
   Hackle: Brown Neck Hackles

3. **Wulff Irresistable**
   Hook: 94840
   Thread: Black
   Tail: White Calf Tail
   Body: Spun Deer Hair clipped to shape
   Wings: White Calf Tail
   Hackle: Brown Neck Hackles

4. **Adams Irresistable**
   Hook: 94840
   Thread: Black
   Tail: Mixed Brown & Grizzly Fibres
   Body: Spun Deer Body Hair clipped to shape
   Wings: Grizzly Hackle Tips
   Hackle: Mixed Brown & Grizzly Neck

COLOR PLATES OF FLIES
(1-7)

Wooly Worm

Montana Nymph

Peacock Nymph

Grey Hackle Peacock

Rio Grande King

Muskrat Nymph

Gold Ribbed Hare's Ear

COLOR PLATES OF FLIES
(8-14)

Brown Bivisible

Grizzly Mosquito

Elk Hair Caddis

Adams

Royal Wulff

Humpy

Muddler Minnow

GLOSSARY

Abdomen.   The back part of a nymph body located between the tail and thorax.

Aft.   The back hackle closest to the bend on a fore and aft fly.

Badger.   A color of hackle feather that ranges from cream to ginger at the ends with a dark center.

Barbule.   The individual fibres of a hackle feather.

Bend.   That part of the hook that curves.

Bobbin.   A fly tying tool used to hold a spool of thread.

Bobbin Threader.   A tool used to thread the bobbin.

Bodkin.   Another name for a dubbing needle.

Brown Red Game.   A color of neck hackle that is brown with a slight reddish tinge.

Butting.   A technique for wrapping material that places each wrap as close to the last wrap as possible without overlapping.

Butts.   The thickest part of the feather or hair. It also refers to material remaining after tying off.

Caddis.   A moth-like aquatic insect. At rest, its wings are folded back over the top of the body in a tent shape, peaking at the center.

Chenille.   A fuzzy strand of fly tying material.

Covert.   A wing case or covering for the body.

Dressing.   The detailing of materials and hook to make a specific fly. Synonymous with Pattern.

Dry Fly.   A fly that when tied is intended to be fished on top of the water.

Dry Fly Hackle.   A technique of wrapping hackles which places the curve of the barbules over the eye. It also refers to the quality of little web and stiff barbules of a hackle.

Dubbing.   The technique of applying a material to a hook that does not lend itself to being wound on a hook. Such as furs.

Dubbing Loop. A technique developed by Poly Rosebrough for dubbing that uses two strands of thread formed in a loop that traps the dubbing material to make dubbing yarn.

Dubbing Needle. A tool, shaped like a needle with a handle, used to pick out dubbing.

Dubbing Wax. A tacky wax used to hold the dubbing material to the thread.

Dun. A light bluish-grey color.

Figure 8. The technique of crisscrossing the thread between the wings to give separation and strength.

Floss. A fly tying material originally made of silk but today is usually made of nylon or acetate. It is packaged in spools with four strands wound together.

Fore. The front hackle on a fore and aft fly.

Furnace. A medium to dark brown color of hackle with a dark center.

Gap. The distance between the hook shank and the hook point.

Ginger. A color of hackle. It ranges from a light ginger or dark cream color to a dark ginger or light brown color.

Grey. A color in the finished fly when grizzly feather is used for material.

Grizzly. The feather from a barred Plymouth Rock rooster. It is light grey with dark bars.

Guard Hairs. Long stiff hairs from muskrat, beaver or other fur.

Hackle. The individual barbules that stand out from the hook shank after they have been wound on.

Hackle Tip. The topmost part of a hackle feather used for wings.

Half Hitch. A knot used in fly tying to temporarily secure the thread to the hook.

Hair Stacker. A tool used to stack hair so that the tips are even.

Head. The part of the fly immediately in back of the eye.

Herl. The long fuzzy strands attached to the tail quills of a peacock or ostrich.

Jam Knot. A knot in which the thread is overlapped when attached to the hook. It is the first step when starting to tie a fly.

Mat. The dubbing material after it has been prepared and is ready to dub onto the thread.

May Fly. The classic aquatic insect with upright wings, and an upcurving body and split tail.

Mottled. A mixed brown color similar to camouflage.

Mylar Tinsel. A synthetic material that is in a strip form. It is shiny with gold on one side and silver on the other.

Neck. The head and neck of a rooster with feathers left on skin.

Noodle. A technique developed by Poly Rosebrough for loop dubbing.

Nymph. The larvae or nymph stage of an aquatic insect.

Palmer. A type of hackle wrap that covers the body or part of the body. It is characterized by space between each wrap.

Pattern. This is a synonym for fly or dressing. It also refers to the specific materials and order of application as in dressing.

Positive Pressure. The amount of pressure applied on the thread to provide a snug wrap without undue pressure or pull.

Prepare. To strip, cut, or select the material to be tied on the hook.

Pre-waxed. A description of modern thread or monocord that has had a coating of wax applied to the entire spool length in order to give the thread some purchase when tying materials to the hook.

Primary. The foremost flight feathers of a bird's wing.

Poly. An abbreviation for polypropelene. It is also a synonym for many synthetics.

Quill. The center of a feather that is attached to the skin. It also may refer to a stripped peacock herl.

Rib. A spaced winding over the body, usually with tinsel or a contrasting wrap.

Saddle. This refers to the location on the rooster where the feather is attached to the skin. It is a long feather used primarily for palmering and longer hackle wraps.

Secondary. The feather from a bird's wing that forms the bulk of the wing. Characteristically with the quill more or less in the center of the feather.

Spade. This refers to the shape of a hackle. It may be from the saddle or neck. It is much wider at the bottom than at the top.

Standard Shank. It is neither long nor short shank. The length will equal one and one-half times the hook gap.

Starting Position. The point where most flies are started. If the bobbin is hanging free, the thread will fall between the barb and the point of the hook.

Stone Fly. A relatively large aquatic insect, hatching primarily in the spring. The stone fly makes up a large portion of a trout's springtime diet. It may be fished in nymph form any time of the year.

Streamer. A fly tied to suggest or imitate a smaller fish. Trout are carnivorous feeders and will feed on any fish smaller than themselves.

Tail. The extension of the hook shank that provides the rear flotation medium in a dry fly.

Thorax. The front part of a nymph or dry fly. It may be equated to a chest area.

Thread. Usually a 6/0 twisted nylon thread used in fly tying. However, the term also refers to monocord, silk, or any other type of material used to attach materials to the hook.

Tie In. The process of attaching materials to the hook shank.

Tinsel. A synthetic material in strip form. It is shiny with gold on one side and silver on the other.

Tippet. In fly tying it is a barbule. Usually it refers to a thicker barbule like those found on the golden pheasant.

Tying Off. After the materials have been tied in and wrapped on the hook, they are tied off with thread, fixing both ends to the shank.

Underfur. That portion of an animal's fur that is closest to the skin.

Underbody. It is that area beneath the body. It is sometimes visible as in the Humpy or invisible as in lead weighting.

Vise. A fly tying tool used to hold the hook firmly.

Web. The darker part of the hackle feather closest to the quill that prevents separation of the barbules.

Wedge. A mass of thread tied to hold some materials like wings in place.

Weighting. A process that uses lead wire to provide extra weight for a fly.

Wet Fly. A fly tied to sink and fish below the surface of the water. It has a distinctive down wing form.

Wet Fly Hackle. A hackle that is wrapped so that the natural curve of the feather is back toward the bend of the hook. It also refers to a softer, poor quality of feather that is unusable when tying dry flies.

Whip Finish. The knot used to finish a fly. It buries the end of the thread under several wraps to ensure that the thread does not unwrap.

Wing. On a fly, a wing is that material applied to suggest the wing of an insect. It also refers to many different materials such as a turkey wing.

Wing Case. That part of a nymph that is usually tied over the thorax to suggest the cased wings of a developing nymph.

Wrap. To tie around the hook.

X Wrap. The figure 8 wrap used to secure and fix wings in place.

INDEX OF PATTERNS